D1066231

THE NASCAR® VAULT

THE NASCAR® VAULT

AN OFFICIAL HISTORY FEATURING RARE COLLECTIBLES FROM MOTORSPORTS IMAGES AND ARCHIVES™

H.A. BRANHAM & BUZ MCKIM

becker&mayer!BOOKS

Copyright © 2004 H.A. Branham and Buz McKim

All rights reserved. No part of this book may be reproduced in any form without written permission from the publisher.

NASCAR is a registered trademark of the National Association for Stock Car Auto Racing.

Library of Congress Control Number: 2004107401

ISBN: 0-9700346-1-X

Printed in China

Design: Todd Bates
Editorial: Conor Risch
Image Research: Shayna Ian
Production Coordination: Leah Finger
Project Management: Sheila Kamuda

All images and historic memorabilia are courtesy of Motorsports Images and Archives, used with permission.

becker&mayer! would like to thank Eddie Roche and Nancy Kendrick from
Motorsports Images and Archives and Buz McKim at NASCAR for their kind help in providing images for this project.

10   9   8   7   6   5   4   3   2

becker&mayer! Books
11010 Northup Way
Bellevue, Washington 98004

www.beckermayer.com

OPPOSITE: The field cruises into Turn 1 at
Richmond International Raceway during a pace
lap under the lights (2001).
OVERLEAF: NASCAR's founders pose for what has become
an historic photo atop Daytona Beach's Streamline Hotel
in December, 1947.

CONTENTS

Bill France Sr.

Bill France

Brian Z. France

Dear NASCAR Fan,

One of the best things about being the chairman and CEO of NASCAR is having my name listed alongside the two men who preceded me in our company's main leadership role—my father and grandfather, Bill France and Bill France Sr.

Those two men laid the groundwork of our sport. Whatever we accomplish in the future will be directly attributable, in part, to their hard work, dedication, and vision.

NASCAR is moving fast these days, on and off the track. Our sport has grown tremendously, to the point where sometimes it's hard to imagine the days many years ago when NASCAR was basically a two-man operation run by my grandfather and his right-hand man at the time, Pat Purcell. Of course, a lot of people say the real boss was my grandmother, Annie B. France.

They did it all. And they did it well. And when my father—helped by my mother, Betty Jane France—took over the reins of the company from my grandfather, he followed their lead.

Many people like to say that my grandfather was responsible for creating NASCAR and my father was responsible for growing NASCAR. There is considerable validity in both assessments, but in truth, their roles can't be defined that simply.

But there is one simple concept that both had in common, a concept my father likes to reference via a favorite poem of his, called "Opportunity," by Edward Rowland Sill.

The poem is about a great battle, and how a brave soldier was wounded and lost his weapon. On the edge of the battlefield, a coward had given up the fight, snapped his sword in two, flung it to the ground, and run away.

The coward's sword was crude and blunt—nothing like the precision blue-steel blade the brave soldier had lost. But when the brave soldier came upon that sword half-buried in the dirt, he snatched it up and carried on the fight.

Here's how Sill put it:

". . . with battle-shout, lifted afresh, he hewed his enemy down, and saved a great cause that heroic day."

In simple terms, the soldier saw an opportunity and made the most of it.

That was the way both my father and grandfather approached opportunities: decisively—and bravely.

We need to remember those days, the battles they fought and the opportunities they sought—and then maximized to the betterment of NASCAR.

And we should always acknowledge how important those days were to building what we enjoy today.

NASCAR has a rich history, one that has been told and retold countless times in words and pictures. *The NASCAR Vault*, you'll find, takes the storytelling process one step further by giving readers replicas of various memorabilia from our sport's past.

Enjoy.

Sincerely,

Brian Z. France
NASCAR Chairman/CEO

1951 LOGO

This is actually the original NASCAR logo unveiled in 1948. Bill France Sr. had a hand in designing it. The cars are based on Frank Lockhart's streamlined Stutz Black Hawk land-speed-record car, which raced on Daytona Beach in 1928.

NASCAR INTERNATIONAL LOGO NUMBER ONE

This logo was used from the mid 1950s through the early 1960s.

1954 NASCAR LOGO

The look of the logo varied a bit from year to year in the early 1950s.

NASCAR INTERNATIONAL LOGO NUMBER TWO

This logo was used from the 1960s through the introduction of the current logo in 1976.

CURRENT LOGO

In the mid 1970s it was time to update the logo. It had to have its own identity as opposed to the sameness of the stick-and-ball sports' logos. A multi-colored "bar" logo was adopted in 1976 and has been the official mark since.

THE FOUNDATION:

CHAPTER ONE

1936-1949

William Henry Getty France brought his young family and his fledgling dreams to Daytona Beach, Florida, in 1934. Driving southward from his hometown of Washington, D.C., he established roots on a whim.

ABOVE: Competitors practice for the inaugural Daytona Beach stock car race in 1936. The cars are entering the north turn, which carried them off the beach and onto State Road A1A.
OPPOSITE: Big Bill France, 1939.

France stopped in Daytona instead of his planned destination, south Florida. An auto mechanic by trade, he first worked in the area as a sign painter before getting a job as a brake specialist at a local Oldsmobile dealership.

Despite the difficulties of life during the Great Depression, France envisioned something special in his future, perhaps involving auto racing, an activity he already had come to enjoy as both a driver and a mechanic.

France was a dreamer, destined to become an achiever. He chose the right community in which to settle. The Daytona Beach area had seen its share of visionaries.

Several miles to the north of Daytona lay Ormond Beach, once a key stop on legendary developer Henry Flagler's railroad system, which lined Florida's east coast and linked the Florida Keys with the continental United States. Flagler's development plan was two-fold, involving railroad tracks and elaborate hotels at each town where the tracks were laid. One of his hallmark hotels was the Hotel Ormond, the largest wooden structure in the world at that time.

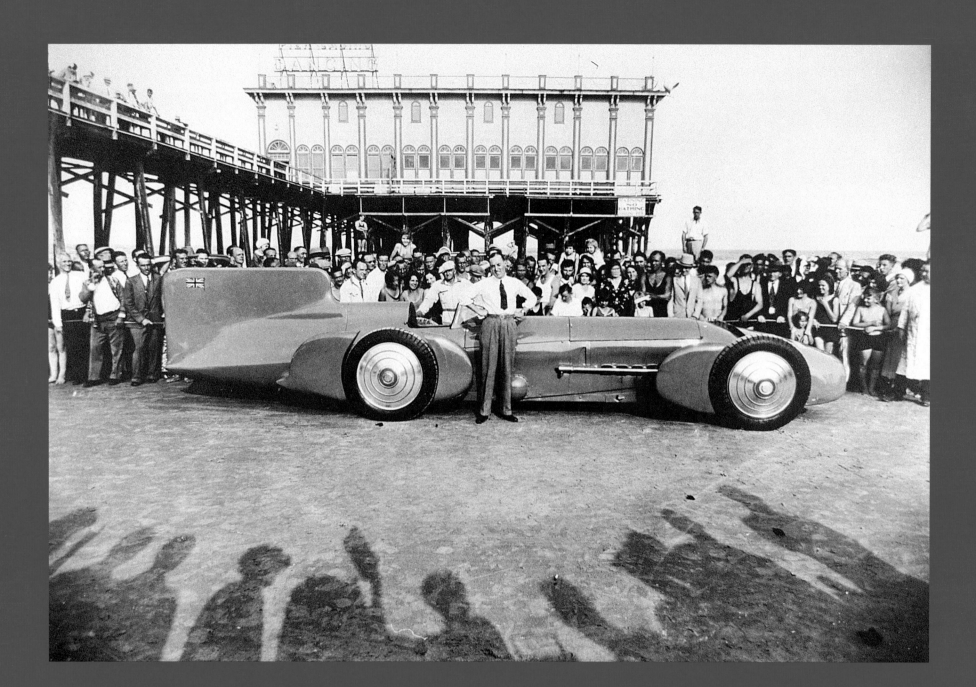

"The birthplace of speed," the sleepy town on the Atlantic Ocean had come to be known as shortly after the turn of the century. Its sands, hard-packed by sun and time, had beckoned to men and their quest for speed.

They came with their outlandish machines from around the world in the early 1900s, lodging mostly at the grand Hotel Ormond on the Halifax River. Men such as Ransom Olds, Alexander Winton, Henry Ford, Louis Chevrolet, and Barney Oldfield, auto-racing's first true star, came to chase the land-speed record, drag racing on the sand, unaware that they were laying the foundation for Daytona's rich racing heritage and establishing a precedent that would, years later, inspire a man whose six-foot-five stature served as a metaphor for his dreams.

William Henry Getty France would soon come to be known simply as "Big Bill" France. But there was nothing simple about what was about to transpire.

Single-car or several-car runs in the pursuit of speed had their place in auto racing lore, but for France, true competition required something more than a single machine against the clock. The future of auto racing was dramatic, door-to-door dueling involving harrowing turns, multiple cars, many contenders, and inevitable contact. That is what kept competitors coming back for more and convinced spectators to shell out their precious, hard-earned

OPPOSITE: Sir Malcolm Campbell proudly poses in front of Daytona's Pier Casino prior to his record beach run in 1932.
TOP: Englishman Kaye Don came to Daytona Beach in 1930 with the Sunbeam Silver Bullet, the longest car ever to race on the beach. Unfortunately, Mr. Don did not set a speed record.
RIGHT: Campbell's Bluebird 5 arrives in Daytona Beach in 1935. This car would be the last to set the World Land Speed Record on Daytona Beach.

250-MILE NATIONAL CHAMPIONSHIP STOCK CAR BEACH-ROAD RACE

DAYTONA BEACH FLORIDA MAR 8 '36

DON J EMERY

dollars to watch and live out vicariously some racing dreams of their own.

In January and February 1936, Big Bill France helped former racer Sig Haugdahl design and build Daytona Beach's first beach-road course for a race sponsored by the city. On race day—March 8—France hopped into a Ford and finished fifth in the 250-mile event, wearing a football helmet as crude protection for a mind that would build a recreational activity into one of America's most popular sports. The city of Daytona lost over $20,000 on the event, which effectively ended the civic venture into auto racing.

The Elks Club of Daytona Beach staged a race in 1937, and that event failed to turn a profit as well, casting a dark cloud over the prospects of future events in the area. Undaunted, France joined forces in February of 1938 with a local businessman named Charlie Reese, and the two promoted a beach-road race of their own. It went well, more or less, as they split a profit of $200. They had made no real money, but they hadn't lost money either, which was more than the city of Daytona or the Elks Club could say for themselves. Encouraged, France and Reese promoted another event that year held on Labor Day. This time they were able to split over $2,000, a more serious profit.

It was a big year for Big Bill—he also worked on a pit crew at the Indianapolis 500. Being involved first hand in auto racing's biggest event fueled France's resolve to find his own permanent niche in the sport.

The onset of World War II halted Daytona's racing just when it was starting to gain in popularity. Racing

Program from Daytona Beach's first stock car race in 1936.

THIS IS NOT A STAY IN PASS
AND
IS NOT GOOD FOR GATE ADMISSION

BILL FRANCE'S
1938 INDY PIT PASS

This is the pass issued to Bill France Sr. when he was a crewmember for a team entered in the 1938 Indianapolis 500.

the night of May 29, 1938.

SAFETY DIRECTOR

1948
RULES AND SPECIFICATIONS
★

NASCAR RULEBOOK

A copy of the first ever NASCAR rulebook. You can see that racing was much less complicated back then.

COMMISSIONER
E. G. "Cannonball" Baker — Indianapolis, Indiana

BOARD OF GOVERNORS
President
Bill France — Daytona Beach, Florida
Promoters
Eddie Bland — Jacksonville, Florida
Bill Tuthill — Hartford, Connecticut
Owners

REPRESENTATIVE RACE REPORT

Name of Track
City or Town
State
Date
Name of Promoter or Manager
NASCAR Representative in Charge of Event
Amount of Prize Money $
Championship Point Fund $
Benevolent Fund $
Total Number of Cars Entered

FIRST EVER
RACE REPORT

The first NASCAR-sanctioned event was held on Daytona Beach in 1948. This is a reproduction of the official race report for that event. Everything was handwritten in the days before hi-tech office equipment.

"We didn't know until qualifying time if the beach was going to be rough or smooth.

WE KNEW THAT WE'D HAVE TO WAIT UNTIL THE TIDE WAS HALFWAY OUT BEFORE WE COULD TELL IF IT WAS DECENT TO RUN ON.

There was no other way. Then we had to worry about the wind, because if it changed, it could affect how far out the tide would go, and how fast it would come in."

—BILL FRANCE SR. ON EARLY BEACH RACING

TOP: Milt Marion, winner of Daytona's first stock car race.
BOTTOM: Jack Rutherfurd in the boat-tail Auburn he drove at Daytona in 1936.
RIGHT: Line up of entrants for the first Daytona Beach stock car race.

ENTRANTS

CAR NO.	MAKE	DRIVER	ENTRANT	QUALIFYING SPEED
14	FORD	WALTER JOHNSON	O. L. MOODY	63.92
5	DODGE	WM. SCHINDLER	H. ATKINSON	59.65
22	FORD	"HICK" JENKINS	H. R. DIXON	67.95
19	FORD	SAM. PURVIS	SAM. PURVIS	67.25
15	FORD	DAN MURPHY	CARL PURSER	63.96
17	FORD	ED. ENG	DON SUTTLE	64.28
29	AUBURN	JOHN RUTHERFORD	JOHN RUTHERFORD	65.97
16	FORD	ALBERT CUSICK	ALBERT CUSICK	64.25
9	FORD	WM. LAWRENCE	WM. LAWRENCE	62.81
11	FORD	LOU CAMPBELL	L. S. CAMPBELL	63.32
21	FORD	BILL SOCKWELL	BILL SOCKWELL	
3	CHEVROLET	B. J. GIBSON	B. J. GIBSON	61.47
1	WILLYS 77	LANGDON QUIMBY	LANGDON QUIMBY	58.71
4	WILLYS 77	SAM COLLIER	SAM COLLIER	58.60
24	FORD	DOC. MACKINZIE	G. D. MACKENZIE	67.92
18	FORD	BEN SHAW	ED. PARKINSON	66.01
6	FORD	BOB SALL	RUDY ADAMS	61.51
26	FORD	TOMMY ELMORE	THOS. ELMORE, JR.	62.30
20	OLDSMOBILE 8	KEN. SCHROEDER	FLOYD A. SMITH	66.32
2	AUBURN	BILL CUMMINGS	M. J. BOYLE	70.39
25	FORD	AL WHEATLEY	AL. WHEATLEY	65.23
12	FORD	AL PIERSON	AL. PIERSON	63.54
27	FORD	JACK HOLLY	JACK HOLLY	68.04
28	FORD	VIRGIL MATHIS	DAN H. STODDARD	66.28
8	FORD	GILBERT FARRELL	C. A. HARDY	62.71
7	LINCOLN ZEPHYR	MAJOR A. T. G. GARDNER	A. T. G. GARDNER	61.76
10	FORD	WILLIAM FRANCE	ISAAC BLAIR	63.02
23	FORD	MILTON MARION	MILT MARION	66.16

— FLAG SIGNALS —

GREEN	Start of Race; Course is clear.
YELLOW	Caution; Bring car under control and reduce speed to 50 miles per hour.
ORANGE with BLUE CENTER	Competitor is attempting to overtake you
WHITE	Report at your pit on the next lap.
RED	Danger; stop.
BLUE	You are entering your last lap.
CHECKER	You have finished.

1936 NATIONAL CHAMPIONSHIP
BEACH AND ROAD RACE
DAYTONA BEACH, FLORIDA

ABOVE: Cars roar down State Road A1A during the 1937 Daytona Beach stock car race.
OPPOSITE: Bill France Sr. finished fifth at Daytona in 1936, driving this 1935 Ford coupe.

finally resumed there in June 1946. But France, who during the war worked as a foreman at Daytona Beach Boat Works, a shipyard that built small, fast boats called "sub-chasers," had returned to the racing business before '46. Just weeks after Japan's summer of 1945 surrender, France was back at it, promoting a race at the fairgrounds in Charlotte, North Carolina, an event he dubbed a "national championship." Considering the number of stock car racing promoters operating at the time, the label was considered ambi-tious, which of course it was. France, though, was in the process of redefining the word "ambition."

Next stop: the Streamline Hotel.

The photograph has become famous—an image as synonymous with NASCAR history as the photo-fin-ish shot, taken at the first Daytona 500, that took three days to decipher and eventually awarded the victory to Lee Petty. The photograph, from December 14, 1947, is of a classic, smoke-filled room packed with twenty-four

faces—one belonging to the soon-to-be monarch of stock car racing in the United States—seated around tables jammed together to simulate a conference-room setting. The photo was taken at a four-day meeting held at the nondescript Streamline Hotel across Highway A1A from the Atlantic Ocean in Daytona Beach, where Big Bill France convinced a cantankerous group consisting of other racing promoters, drivers, mechanics, and assorted VIPs that a unified sanctioning body was essential for the long-term growth of stock car racing.

At the meeting, France spoke for the first time what have become the bywords of modern-day NASCAR: cost containment, safety, and entertainment value. He wanted a circuit of cars the average person could relate to, but that were also eye-catching. "Strictly Stock" was the label France envisioned.

The Streamline meeting is remembered as a gathering at which France gave a lengthy, stream-of-consciousness type of lecture, during which he made a stunning prophecy:

We don't know how big stock car racing can be . . . but I do know that if stock car racing is handled properly, it can go the way Big Car racing has gone.

"Big Car" was code for Indy cars and auto racing's premier event, the Indianapolis 500. Already France was shooting for the moon.

The concept of a sanctioning body was agreed to relatively easily compared to the haggling that went on about the organization's title. After several suggestions,

TOP: Harold Grant spins out coming into the south turn at Daytona Beach during an early stock car race.
BOTTOM: Atlanta's Raymond Parks strikes a somber pose on Daytona Beach. He was racing's first multicar team owner. Bill France Sr. drove for him prior to World War II.

**WE HAD TO COME UP WITH A NAME.**
Red Byron wanted National Stock Car Racing
Association (NSCRA). Red Vogt suggested . . .
National Association for Stock Car Auto
Racing (NASCAR) . . . Then somebody pointed
out that there already was an association in
Georgia with the NSCRA name, so Ed Bruce
moved to disregard the first name and incor-
porate, in Florida, under the name of National
Association for Stock Car Auto Racing. Jack
Peters seconded, and it became the official
name of the new organization.**"**

—BILL TUTHILL RECALLING NASCAR'S ORGANIZATIONAL MEETING IN 1947[2]

STREAMLINE HOTEL, DAYTONA BEACH, FLORIDA

FRANCE'S WORDS LOOM PROPHETIC

On December 14, 1947, during an organizational meeting at the Streamline Hotel in Daytona Beach, Florida, the National Association for Stock Car Auto Racing (NASCAR) was born. At the meeting, NASCAR's founder and soon-to-be first president, Bill France, addressed the future of a then-fledgling sport. A portion of his statements from that day now adorn a wall in the NASCAR Research and Development Center in Concord, North Carolina.

France's words loom prophetic, more than half a century later.

"Stock car racing has got distinct possibilities for Sunday shows and we do not know how big it can be if it's handled properly. ... It can go the same way as Big Car racing. I believe stock car racing can become a nationally recognized sport by having a National Point Standing. Stock car racing as we've been running it is not, in my opinion, the answer. ..... We must try to get track owners and promoters interested in building stock car racing up. We are all interested in one thing that is, improving the present conditions. The answer lies in our group right here today to do it."

Red Vogt, one of the top mechanics of his day, tossed out "National Association for Stock Car Auto Racing."

NASCAR.

It stuck.

Two months later NASCAR staged its first race on the new beach-road course located approximately ten miles south of Daytona Beach in the town of Ponce Inlet. The new 2.2-mile course replaced the older 3.2-mile course, which was located eight miles north in what is now the town of Daytona Beach Shores. The move was made at the request of the Oceanfront Cottage Association due to continued development along the beachfront. Both courses used the beach and a section of State Road A1A. They were, without question, the most unique race tracks in the world.

The inaugural NASCAR race, dubbed the Edward Rayson Memorial, was run on February 15, 1948, a week before NASCAR was incorporated. Word had spread throughout the racing world of the new sanctioning body.

Bill France had gained trust among racers through his years of promoting events in an honest manner. He had no problem attracting entrants for the big race. Big Bill stated, "We have sixty-two entries from twelve different states. It's the largest number of entries ever made for a stock car race in this country. We expect at least fifty of them to compete."

LEFT: The Streamline Hotel on A1A in Daytona Beach. The little room on top of the building was the birthplace of NASCAR. **OPPOSITE:** The original founders of NASCAR. Big Bill France and NASCAR secretary Bill Tuthill are seated at the head of the table. Sam Packard, third from the right, seated with hands folded, was the last surviving member of this group. He passed away in March 2003.

——FIRST NASCAR SANCTIONED RACE IN 1948——

8TH ANNUAL

DAYTONA BEACH

MODIFIED

STOCK CAR CLASSIC

Sunday, February 15, 1948

150-Mile Race on the New 2.2-Mile Stock Car Championship Road-Beach Course

National Association for **STOCK CAR** *AUTO RACING* INC.

NASCAR

NATIONAL HEADQUARTERS, 29 GOODALL AVE., DAYTONA BEACH, FLORIDA
PRESIDENT—BILL FRANCE   COMMISSIONER—E. G. "CANNONBALL" BAKER

— Affiliates —

AMERICAN STOCK CAR RACING ASSOCIATION, INC. — TRENTON, N. J.
OHIO SPEEDWAY ASSOCIATION, INC. — BEREA, OHIO
CHATTANOOGA RACING ASSOCIATION — CHATTANOOGA, TENN.

— Racing Classification —

STRICTLY STOCK • MODIFIED STOCK • ROADSTERS

"AUTO RACING THAT IS OPEN TO EVERYONE"

Why not join an association that gives every one an opportunity to take part in the country's growing sport of stock car racing? We welcome all those who want to become part of a national organization. Competition memberships and associate memberships open to all persons who drive an automobile. You may be eligible for NASCAR sanctioned events which include: Speed Trials on Daytona Beach—Racing on the new Road-Beach Course—Sanctioned races on all types of tracks—National Roadster Championship on Daytona Beach.

FOR FULL INFORMATION WRITE TODAY TO NATIONAL HEADQUARTERS

Among the cars entered were the potent Fords of Atlanta, Georgia's Raymond Parks. His team was considered the finest in the nation, and they were always the cars to beat.

"I always came with three cars," Parks said. "Red Byron drove one, Bob Flock drove one, and I would occasionally drive the third one. I was listed as a driver in that first race, but Bob Flock actually drove the car. He finished third, and Red won the thing.

"I recall it was a bit chilly that day, as it usually is in Daytona in February. The beach was smooth, but the north turn broke up where the dirt met the asphalt of A1A. Other than that, the track conditions seemed good."

Parks always had the best equipment, best mechanics, and best drivers. Among them was Bill France Sr.

"Big Bill drove for me before the war," Parks said. "One of my cars, a Graham, really went with Bill behind the wheel. We raced throughout the South and also at Langhorne, Pennsylvania. We won a lot of races."

Parks was the forerunner of current team owners such as Rick Hendrick and Jack Roush, who field impressive multicar teams. He spent a small fortune on racing and was one of the key people who helped get NASCAR off the ground—starting with that first race on the sands.

A crowd of 14,000 paid $2.50 apiece to watch the historic event, which began at 3:30 p.m. with a staggered start. The race officials were fearful of a major first-turn pileup, so they let each row of cars go at one-second intervals from a standing start.

Advertisement for NASCAR's first race.

BEACH-ROAD RACE TICKET

Racing seemed to be a bit of a bargain back in 1939 as witnessed by the cost on this ticket. Most of the spectator areas at the old Daytona beach-road course were standing room only. Very few bleachers existed at the time.

FIRST STRICTLY STOCK RACE PROGRAM

NASCAR introduced the Strictly Stock division, which today is known as the NASCAR Nextel Cup Series. The first event was held at the Charlotte, North Carolina, three-quarter-mile dirt track on June 19, 1949.

OFFICIAL PAYOFF SHEET

Payoff sheets were written in pencil back in 1948 just in case there was a dispute in a driver's finishing position and amount of winnings. This sheet is signed by Joe Epton, who later became the head of NASCAR Timing and Scoring. Epton still lives in the Daytona Beach area.

ABOVE: North-turn action during NASCAR's first race in 1948.
OPPOSITE: Robert "Red" Byron, NASCAR's first champion, seen here in Victory Lane after the inaugural NASCAR race.

Among the entrants were 1947 national champion Fonty Flock, his older brother Bob, and the youngest Flock brother, Tim.

Future stars Curtis Turner, Jim Paschal, Fireball Roberts, and Buck Baker were also part of the field of fifty-six drivers taking the green flag. Daytona's very own Marshall Teague led the first ever lap of NASCAR competition.

The field found the south turn the most difficult portion of the course. It was very tight, and if negotiated incorrectly, it would send a car sailing over the sand bank past a rickety wooden observation tower filled with wide-eyed observers, for a drop of some ten to fifteen feet.

Nearly a dozen competitors ended their hopes of a win by going over the south-turn banking.

Race favorite Fonty Flock seemed to have victory in his grasp with a half-mile lead and just eighteen laps to go when his Ford snapped a spindle, sending it and him flipping into the backstretch palmetto scrubs. This incident handed the lead to Teague, but Red Byron, in the Parks Ford, was closing fast. The two drivers were nose to tail on Lap 50 as they came upon Mickey Rhodes in the north turn. Byron went to the outside with momentum on his side. Teague dove to the inside but got bogged down in the soft sand. Red Byron took the lead by

It took fans
to claim this tr...

Ray Hall   March
Red Byron   April
Red Byron   Janu...
Red Byron   19...

SOUVENIR AUTOGRAPH PROGRAM
Ninth Annual Championship
200-Mile Stock Car Race

Daytona Beach, Florida
Over the Famous Beach-Road Course
Sunday, January 16, 1949 -- PRICE 50c

thirty yards coming out of the turn onto the paved backstretch, and remained in the lead for the rest of the race. Marshall Teague finished second, some fifteen seconds behind Byron.

The Byron-Parks team took home a whopping $1,000 for winning the 149.6-mile affair. It was Byron's third straight victory in Daytona. While standing in the makeshift Victory Lane, Byron exclaimed, "This is the hardest race I ever won in Daytona Beach. I had to work all the way. Teague was stiff competition. I was lucky to catch him. He ran out of brakes and I was plain lucky. I've always said the car is 90 percent of winning. The driver and luck take care of the other 10 percent."

Byron's mechanic was the premier "wrench turner" of the day, Louis "Red" Vogt, the man who suggested the name "NASCAR" at the organizational meeting in December 1947.

Looking back on that historic event, Raymond Parks stated, "No one realized what they were seeing that day. The way NASCAR has grown is amazing. No one had any idea of it getting as big as it has."

LEFT: Program from the 1949 Daytona Beach stock car race.
OPPOSITE: NASCAR stars of 1949. Clockwise from left: Tim Flock; Harold Kite and his car owner, Carl Green; Curtis Turner; and Bob Flock.
PAGE 33: Red Byron is congratulated by his mechanic, Buckshot Morris, and a crowd of fans after an early win.

" No one realized what they were seeing that day.

THE WAY NASCAR HAS GROWN IS AMAZING.

No one had any idea of it getting as big as it did. **"**

—RAYMOND PARKS ON NASCAR'S INAUGURAL RACE[3]

THE

CHAPTER TWO

1950s

DIRT TO ASPHALT, SHORT TRACK TO SUPERSPEEDWAY

When pondering the "distinct" possibilities big-time stock car racing offered, Bill France Sr. eventually set his sights on bigger—and faster—race tracks. Big Bill was thinking big, which meant advancing racing beyond the novelty category.

And while dirt-track racing was undeniably exciting, it too had inherent limitations, mainly in terms of image. It must be remembered that from the outset, NASCAR was chasing the image of Indianapolis, a place where a crude-brick racing surface had been replaced by pavement. NASCAR's evolution from dirt tracks to pavement and/or concrete was only natural as France sought to grow his sport.

To this day, dirt-track proponents have a saying:

"Dirt's for racing; asphalt's for getting there."

Big Bill France did not subscribe to that saying, but he did agree, more or less, with its latter portion. Asphalt was indeed for "getting there," meaning it was the type of surface that would lead NASCAR to the next level.

That fact became obvious to France after the 1950 inaugural running of the Southern 500 at Darlington (South Carolina) International Raceway. The future of NASCAR—five-hundred-mile events on banked, paved, oval tracks—was displayed in startling fashion.

Sand, dirt, clay, whatever—all seemed suddenly obsolete.

PAGE 34: Bill France Sr., in rear wearing a dark jacket, converses with flagman Johnny Bruner Sr. before the 1955 Daytona Beach stock car race.
LEFT: Miss NASCAR poses with an old beach landmark in 1956.
OPPOSITE: A pack of cars roar through the north turn during the 1955 Daytona Beach stock car event. Curtis Turner, in his white and black No. 99 Oldsmobile, takes to the outside while Dick Joslin, in the orange Buick, brings up the rear.

CURTIS TURNER IN PITS
DARLINGTON SPEEDWAY

SOUTHERN 500
STEEPED IN HISTORY

Other professional sports have their "majors." Golf and tennis, for example, group their four biggest events into a "Grand Slam." Following the lead of the country-club sports, NASCAR established its own set of four "majors." And it all started with the Southern 500.

On September 4, 1950, Darlington International Raceway in Darlington, South Carolina, hosted the first Southern 500. Darlington was a new and unique egg-shaped oval built by Harold Brasington, a Darlington resident who had fallen in love with auto racing after attending the 1938 Indianapolis 500.

Brasington's friends understood his interest in the intriguing sport. But some didn't understand how that translated into actually building a superspeedway.

"Most folks around [Darlington] thought Harold had lost his mind," recalled lifelong Darlington resident Harold King.

The 1.25-mile track's puzzling configuration, which would become a key component of Darlington lore, resulted from limitations imposed by the original acreage. An adjacent plot was home to a fishpond and the owner wouldn't sell. So to fit the track on his land, Brasington had to narrow the area of Turn 2. The result was Darlington International Raceway's famous egg shape.

Oddly, the more normal configuration at the track's other end became notorious because cars repeatedly scraped the outside retaining wall coming out of Turn 4. Therein was the origin of the "Darlington stripe," the badge of honor in the form of scraped-off paint worn by cars on their right side. (In the 1990s, the start-finish line was moved to the opposite straight, and Darlington began to apply the stripe to cars as they came out of Turn 2.)

"Darlington is special; she's always been special and she always will be," said NASCAR vice president Jim Hunter, the former longtime president of the track—now known as Darlington Raceway.

"One thing has remained constant about Darlington over the years. It is still the meanest, toughest, most unforgiving and unpredictable old track in America. And despite a cosmetic makeover in recent years designed to offer a more fan-friendly atmosphere, Darlington Raceway retains that old appeal and flavor that makes it so special.

"And that's what I've always liked about it. You can feel just how special it is as you walk through the gates. The drivers feel it. The crews and car owners feel it. And of course the fans feel it, also."

Darlington was chosen by Bill France to host America's first 500-mile stock car event—on Labor Day, no less. The choice of date cannot be overlooked or downplayed. It was no coincidence that NASCAR's biggest race had a holiday connection along the lines of the Indianapolis 500's relationship with Memorial Day.

LEFT: Herschel McGriff, No. 52, moves toward the pits during the 1950 Southern 500 at Darlington, South Carolina.
OPPOSITE: Cars roar down Darlington Raceway's front stretch in 1950.

NING UNDER CAUTION FLAG
DARLINGTON SPEEDWAY

SOUVENIR PROGRAM

★ ★ SECOND ANNUAL ★ ★ ★

"SOUTHERN 500"

GRAND NATIONAL CIRCUIT STOCK CAR RACE

DARLINGTON RACEWAY

LABOR DAY
MONDAY
Sept.
3

When it began, the race was NASCAR's longest and richest event, paying a total purse of $25,500. It also had fifteen days of time trials—Brasington's idea, to further pattern his race after Indy's annual May ritual—and a starting field of seventy-five cars, which made for organized mayhem.

Johnny Mantz had the slowest-qualifying car in the field, but at the finish, after six hours and thirty-eight minutes of racing, his 1950 Plymouth took the checkered flag.

Bill Rexford finished fourth, taking over the series points lead that day en route to winning the Grand National championship.

Unfortunately—and perhaps a bit unfairly—Rexford is remembered more as the beneficiary of a NASCAR ruling. During the 1950 season, Bill France slapped substantial point penalties on both Red Byron and Lee Petty for racing in events not sanctioned by NASCAR. Twice Byron had all of his points taken away and had to start from scratch. Petty was dealt that severe punishment once. Chances are one of those drivers would've won the 1950 title rather than Rexford were it not for the penalties.

The first Southern 500 was the highlight of 1950, and the race immediately stood as NASCAR's crown jewel. Eventually it would add status to its résumé, recognized as the initial race in NASCAR's Grand Slam, to be joined through the years by three others.

For years, NASCAR's Grand Slam looked like this: the Daytona 500 (the richest race), the Talladega 500

Program for the 1951 Southern 500. 1950 winner Johnny Mantz graces the cover.

CENTURY CLUB CERTIFICATE

During the annual Speedweeks events on Daytona Beach during the 1950s, a measured mile event was held. It was open to anyone who wanted see "what their machine would do." If a competitor registered a speed of more than one hundred miles per hour, they became a member of The Century Club. A speedometer needle was drawn on the certificate to mark the competitor's speed, hence Mr. French ran a bit more than 110 miles per hour.

Race

ONE OF THE FIRST AUTO RACING-BASED BROCHURES

Today, nearly every track in the country has some form of informational brochure, and this 1952 publication represents the very beginnings of that trend.

Daytona Beach

SPEED WEEK

sponsored by The National Association of Stock Car Auto Racing

February 3-10, 1952

"Without Darlington Raceway, NASCAR might not be where it is today. And without NASCAR, Darlington Raceway would certainly not be where it is today. The two were a perfect match all those years ago, when that first Southern 500 was run. A perfect match indeed—who would've believed it?"

THEY STUNG LIKE A BEE— HORNETS WERE THE FIRST SUPERCARS

In sports car racing there is a favorite saying of promoters, publicists, and over-the-top public-address announcers that emphasizes machinery over man.

"The cars are the stars."

In NASCAR, nothing could be further from the truth. The drivers have always been an important component of the promotional equation. However, the link between fans and car types, and the loyalties involved, have likewise been recognized.

Through the years, various car types have emerged, helping create NASCAR's fundamental appeal. And while these cars may not have been the stars, they certainly have been essential to turning *drivers* into stars.

Instead of *superstars*, call them *supercars*.

For NASCAR, the first supercar was the Hudson Hornet.

The Hornet was the precursor to other supercars that have emerged throughout NASCAR history —Richard Petty's Plymouths of the 1960s; David Pearson's Mercurys of the 1970s; Bill Elliott's Ford Thunderbirds of the 1980s; the Chevrolet Monte

ABOVE: Marshall Teague and crew celebrated after winning the 1951 beach race at Daytona. It was the first major win for NASCAR's first supercar, the Hudson Hornet.
OPPOSITE: Teague in his race-winning car. The front was covered with masking tape to prevent sand from hitting the chrome and paint. This car was essentially a street machine.

(the fastest), the World 600 (the longest), and the Southern 500 (the oldest).

In the 1990s, the Brickyard 400 at Indianapolis nudged its way into this elite group, but obscuring NASCAR's long-standing Grand Slam was a small price to pay for including Indy on the schedule.

"Darlington Raceway has earned its place in NASCAR history," Jim Hunter said. "For one thing, it was 'first'; the very first. There were no other asphalt tracks conducting 500-mile races for stock cars when Darlington was built. And how it was built, of course, is a story in itself, a great story.

NASCAR SUPERCARS

1950s: Hudson Hornet

• **TOP DRIVER:** Herb Thomas

• **OTHER MEMORABLE DRIVERS:**
Dick Rathmann, Marshall Teague,
Tim Flock, Fonty Flock

• **RACES WON:** 79

• **CHAMPIONSHIPS:**
Herb Thomas in 1951 and 1953.
Tim Flock in 1952.

NOTABLE: The Hornet had a very powerful inline, flat-head six-cylinder engine with the famed "Twin H" intake featuring two carburetors. The Hornet was known for its superior handling characteristics due to its low center of gravity. The car had a "step down" floor, meaning the floor pan was set down between the frame rails of the chassis, enabling the car to handle very well.

"Two years after our 1947 NASCAR meeting Harold Brasington started construction of Darlington—the first superspeedway. He was in the gravel business and had a bunch of trucks and tractors. He decided to build the track at Darlington because it was his home . . .

HE SOLD $25,000 WORTH OF ADVANCE TICKETS. IT WAS A BIG RISK AT THE TIME . . .

He was short of drivers, so I took a look at it and was impressed with the effort he made. We brought in NASCAR and the NASCAR drivers and put on the first big race for him. "

—BILL FRANCE SR. ON DARLINGTON RACEWAY AND THE FIRST SOUTHERN 500

Carlos driven by Dale Earnhardt and Jeff Gordon in the 1990s.

From 1951 to 1954, Hudson set the standard for excellence. During that period Hudsons won seventy-nine races, their flat-head six-cylinder engines overachieving, in part, because of superior handling.

Excellent drivers also had something to do with the Hornet's legacy of success—drivers such as Marshall Teague and series champions Herb Thomas and Tim Flock. The Hudson's four-year dominance started with Teague's season-opening victory in 1951, on the 4.1-mile beach-road course in Daytona Beach, Teague's hometown.

Thomas won the 1951 and 1953 championships. Flock was the titlist in 1952. In 1954 Thomas finished as series runner-up behind Lee Petty.

After 1954, Hudsons won only once more in NASCAR's premier series: Thomas in 1955's second race, in West Palm Beach, Florida. But their brief, shining period stands as a landmark in NASCAR's formative years.

TOP: Bill Blair, in his No. 41 Oldsmobile, leads Dick Linder's No. 77 Studebaker during the 1951 Daytona Beach stock car race.
BOTTOM: Race winner Herb Thomas, waving, is joined by his car owner, Marshall Teague (in sport coat), and mechanic Harry Van Driel (center) after his 1952 win at North Wilkesboro, North Carolina.

SNAPSHOT: NASCAR'S SPEEDWAY DIVISION

NASCAR's foray into Indy-style racing was brief, but it sure was intriguing. It was an experiment that didn't quite take. But it attracted considerable interest initially, with many top drivers—people like Fireball Roberts and Buck Baker among them—competing.

In 1952, Bill France saw his new Speedway Division as an alternative to the American Automobile Association–sanctioned Indy Car circuit that included, of course, the Indianapolis 500. France's version called for open-wheel chassis with stock engines. Affordability was the byword.

The new division's first race was held in May at Darlington. Buck Baker won that day, and went on to take the championship in a seven-race season. Here's a keeper of a footnote: Baker's car—except for the stock Cadillac engine mandated by NASCAR rules—was the same car that had won the Indianapolis 500 in 1941 with Mauri Rose at the wheel.

A skeletal schedule of Speedway Division races followed in 1953, with Pete Allen winning the division's championship. By then, low car-counts and sparse crowds had doomed the division, proving that open-wheel racing remained a hard sell in the South.

After the 1953 season, the Speedway cars were history, but they are history worth remembering.

OPPOSITE: NASCAR Speedway Division cars compete at Martinsville Speedway, Virginia, on May 25, 1952.
TOP: The field lines up for the inaugural race of NASCAR's Speedway Division at Darlington in 1952.
BOTTOM: Bill France Sr. in his open-wheeled, pre-NASCAR days.

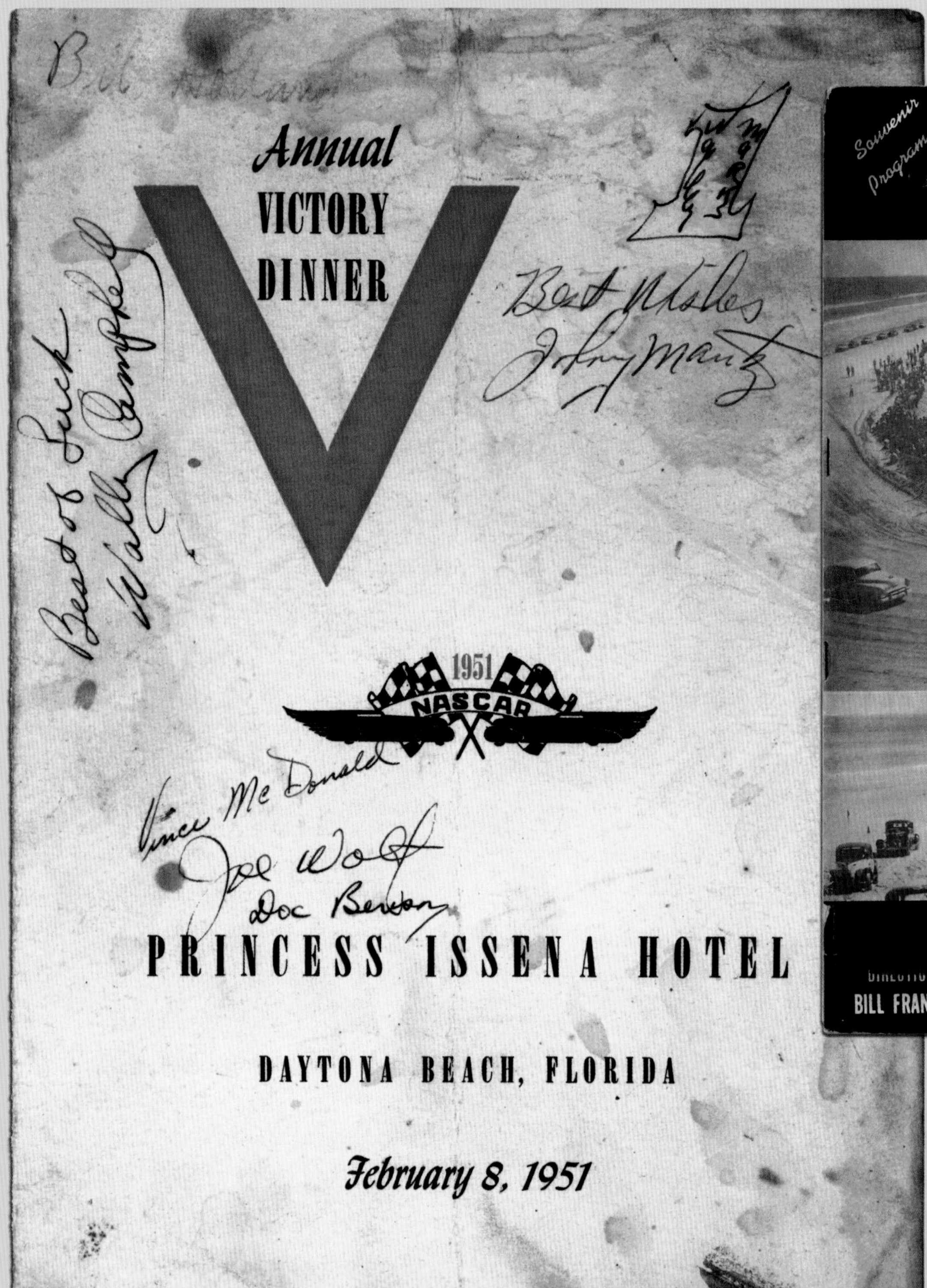

Annual
VICTORY
DINNER

1951
NASCAR

PRINCESS ISSENA HOTEL

DAYTONA BEACH, FLORIDA

February 8, 1951

ANNUAL WINTER
Daytona Beach Classics

Souvenir Program

Golden Anniversary
Daytona Beach Speed Events
1903 - 1953

and Sportsmen's Stock Car R...
SATURDAY, FEBRUARY 14, 1953 - 1:45 P. M.

DIRECTION
BILL FRANCE

160-MILE GRAND NATIONAL CIRCUIT RACE
SUNDAY, FEBRUARY 15, 1953 - 1:45 P. M.

50c

LEFT: Program from 1951 NASCAR awards banquet, featuring signatures of Wally Campbell, Speedway Division driver and early Modified Division star, and Johnny Mantz, winner of the inaugural Southern 500.

ABOVE: Program from the 1953 Daytona Beach stock car race, celebrating years of competition on the beach.

Cylinder head capacity	Min.76 C.C.
Flywheel weight	Min. 7 lbs.
Fuel capacity at filler spout	Max.21 gal.
Rim width	Max. 8 in.
Tires—All 4 must be same size	Max. 15x820
Weight of car	Min. 3974 lbs.
Camshaft No.	6480561
Carburetor No.	6480530
Type lifters	Hydraulic

SECTION 21A
CONVERTIBLE DIVISION

1. Specifications shall follow the same general pattern as for the Grand National Circuit, where applicable, with this exception:

a. All Convertible engines will be limited to one four-barrel carburetor, and any carburetor that is standard production equipment on American manufactured cars may be interchanged if venturi size is no larger than the original carburetor for said make and model.

b. Standard, unaltered four-barrel manifolds for make and model must be used.

PACIFIC COAST LATE MODEL

All Grand National and Short Track engines, both 1956 and 1957 models, competing in the Pacific Coast Divisions (territory in the Mountain and Pacific time zones) will be limited to one four-barrel carburetor and manifolds as permitted in the Convertible Division.

SECTION 21B
SHORT TRACK — LATE MODEL

Short Track Division races are open to 1956 and 1957 models of American-made passenger cars, unless otherwise specified on the entry blank, and will operate under the Grand National Circuit specifications, wherever applicable, with the exception of such changes herein listed:

1. ENGINES

a. Complete engines must be in chassis and body for which they are catalogued.

49

First Annual — **Official Souvenir Program**

NASCAR SANCTIONED — NATIONAL ASSOCIATION FOR STOCK CAR AUTO RACING, INC.

500 MILE
INTERNATIONAL SWEEPSTAKES
AND OTHER RACING EVENTS
Feb. 20, 21, 22-1959

10th Annual Safety and Performance Trials Feb. 15-19, 1959

PRICE $1.00

Daytona International Speedway
"WORLD'S FASTEST AND FINEST RACE COURSE"
DAYTONA BEACH, FLORIDA

SUNDAY, AUGUST 12 – STATE FAIR GROUNDS TRACK

Sponsored by the
SPORTS COMMITTEE FOR DETROIT'S 250th BIRTHDAY FESTIVAL

OFFICIAL PROGRAM 50¢

DON'T FORGET THE MOTOR CITY

NASCAR came to Detroit in 1951 and '52, a monumental occurrence, as those two races truly introduced NASCAR to the city of automobile manufacturers, and no doubt played a role in future factory support of the sport.

And, present day races at Michigan International Speedway notwithstanding, when we say NASCAR came to Detroit, we mean just that: the two races were held a short drive from the city at the Michigan State Fairgrounds.

Tommy Thompson, driving a Chrysler, won the 1951 Motor City 250. The race featured fifteen different car makes. Motor City indeed.

Tim Flock won the 1952 race in a Hudson. His brother Fonty Flock finished last in the field of forty-seven, his Oldsmobile 88 retired after only ten laps because of a busted tie-rod.

KIEKHAEFER: A MAN BEFORE HIS TIME

Multidriver teams and multicar transporters are two staples of modern-day NASCAR racing. It is hard to imagine days without car owners such as Jack Roush, Rick Hendrick, and Richard Childress fielding several cars for the balance of a season. Likewise, it is hard to

LEFT: Program from the 1951 Detroit 250. Many historians feel this event prompted Detroit auto manufacturers to become involved in NASCAR racing.
OPPOSITE: The field cruises past a full house during the pace lap at Detroit, 1951.

ABOVE: Carl Kiekhaefer's racing team of 1956. He was the first car owner to transport his racers to the track in this fashion.

OPPOSITE: Joe Weatherly (No. 12) and Curtis Turner (No. 26) wheel their factory-backed Ford convertibles through the south turn at Daytona in 1956. The historic Ponce Inlet lighthouse, in the background, was a landmark of the early Daytona races.

fathom a garage area without the massive, eighteen-wheeled transporters teams now use to move cars from race to race.

Carl Kiekhaefer was a pioneer of those staples.

Kiekhaefer, his fortune already amassed via the enormous success of his Mercury Outboard boat-engine company, came to NASCAR in 1955. He was at least partially motivated by his desire to further promote his outboards. His massive car haulers, with the words "Mercury Outboards" emblazoned on the side, were the ultimate eye-catching, rolling billboards.

In 1955 Kiekhaefer's drivers, including Grand National champion Tim Flock, won twenty-two races and finished one-two four times. In one event, Kiekhaefer even fielded four cars.

Today that would be no big deal. In 1955 it was groundbreaking.

TOPS DOWN: A BRIEF BUT ILLUSTRIOUS ERA

From 1956 to '59, a colorful portion of NASCAR history was written in the form of the Convertible Division, which resulted from NASCAR's merging with the Indiana-based Society of Autosports Fellowship and Education (SAFE), an organization that already had a convertible class Bill France found interesting.

Beginning in 1956, the Convertible Division's forty-two-race schedule was a playground for a driver with a personality to match the cars. Curtis Turner was flamboyant on and off the track: he drove fast and lived faster. Having made and lost millions of dollars in the timber business, for Turner racing was basically a hobby. He approached it as

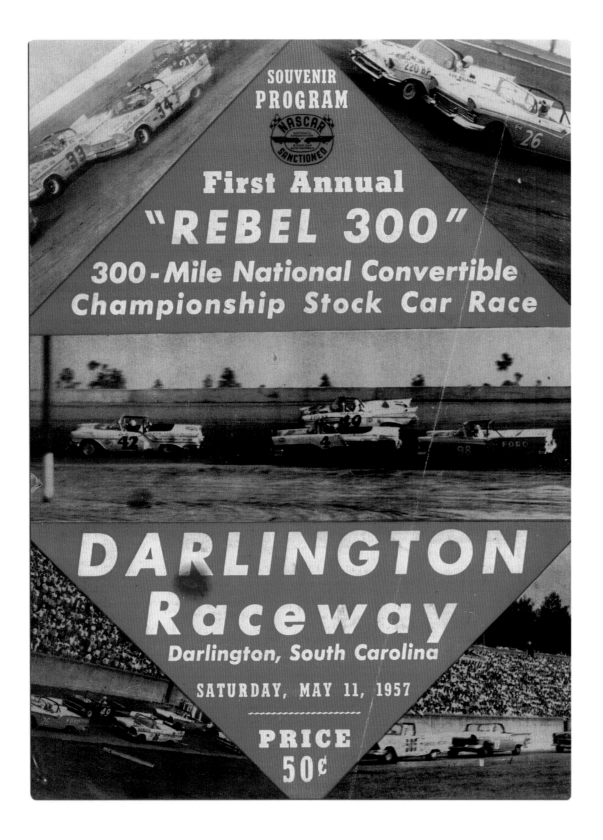

Program from the 1957 Rebel 300 at Darlington. This event was Fireball Roberts' first superspeedway win.

such, which made him as much an entertainer as he was a race contender.

Turner won twenty-two events in 1956, but didn't win the series championship. Under a point system that rewarded consistency, Bob Welborn's thirty-nine top-ten finishes carried him to the first Convertible crown. Welborn also won the series title in 1957 and '58, with Joe Lee Johnson taking the championship in '59, the division's final season.

And how appropriate was this?: The Convertible Division's first event, on February 25, 1956, was contested on the beach-road course in Daytona Beach. Turner won, besting a talent-laden field that included Fireball Roberts, Herb Thomas, Marvin Panch, and Joe Weatherly.

The ragtops went out in style. In the last three races of 1959, the winners were Richard Petty, Lee Petty, and Ned Jarrett. For twenty-two-year-old Richard, it was his first NASCAR victory of any type.

THE APPLES DIDN'T FALL FAR

The 1950s introduced several racing families who proved to be instrumental in establishing NASCAR and helping it evolve into America's number one motorsport.

Lee Petty and Ned Jarrett were two fathers whose great careers would be mirrored—and in some cases exceeded—by their sons. Ditto for Buck Baker and Ralph Earnhardt. It was a veritable phenomenon of the '50s.

 I guess I was 18, 19. I ran a race at Metrolina Fairgrounds on the old dirt track there. I finished 10th. It was midseason when I started, and the last few races I was running second, third. I never won a race that first season.

THE NEXT SEASON I WON THE FIRST RACE AND WENT ON TO WIN 26 OF THEM.

That was on the tracks at Metrolina and Concord, North Carolina.

—DALE EARNHARDT ON HIS FIRST RACE[5]

NASCAR stars of the 1950s and '60s. Clockwise from top left: Lee Petty (1954), Buck Baker (1961), Ralph Earnhardt (1953), and Ned Jarrett (1965).
OPPOSITE: Scene from the 1959 Daytona 500, which featured both sedans and convertibles.

Lee Petty was the first three-time champion of NASCAR's premier series (1954, '58, '59). Son Richard, though, won seven championships, a record still, albeit matched by Dale Earnhardt.

Ned Jarrett began making his name in the 1950s and went on to win two championships in the '60s ('61 and '65). Son Dale won the 1999 title and also has three Daytona 500 victories to his credit. Ned never won NASCAR's biggest race, a major disappointment that was soothed considerably when Dale won the 500 for the first time, in 1993, with television commentator Ned providing the emotional call in the final laps for CBS.

Buck Baker's two championships came in 1956 and '57, making him the first to win titles in consecutive seasons. Son Buddy never won the championship, but he did win nineteen races, and became one of NASCAR's premier drivers in the 1980s.

Ralph Earnhardt made fifty-one starts in NASCAR's premier series. Rather remarkably, he never won, a run of futility that belied his extensive talent. Earnhardt was unquestionably one of the greatest dirt-track racers of all time. Indeed, many historians consider him the very best on dirt and perhaps the best short-track racer in history, period—no matter the surface. Utilizing an aggressive style that would be adopted by his son Dale, Ralph did capture the championship in NASCAR's Sportsman Division—the forerunner to today's NASCAR Busch Series, the nation's number two motorsports series—in 1956.

Ralph's talent has been recognized repeatedly since his death in 1973 at the age of forty-five. In 1989 he was inducted into the National Motorsports Press Association Hall of Fame. In 1997 he was inducted

CAN YOU IMAGINE?

The 1959 Daytona 500 was known as a "sweepstakes" race. The sweepstakes designation was assigned to a race in which standard Grand National sedans made up part of the field and entries from the NASCAR Convertible division made up the rest. This was common practice for many NASCAR races in the late 1950s.

Legendary driver Marvin Panch had an interesting story concerning Daytona's only "sweepstakes 500." He arrived at the track with a 1958 Ford hardtop, ready for action. Big Bill France came down to the pits and explained to the drivers that the field was short of convertibles. He said that if anyone would cut the roof off his car and enter as a convertible, Big Bill would pay him a $500 bonus. Panch thought the $500 offer sounded pretty good, so he lit his cutting torch, and the Ford immediately shed its lid.

Once on the track, Panch began to wonder if he had made the right decision. The car was quite a bit slower than the hardtops, and the air swirling around gave him the feeling he was being sucked out of the No. 98 Ford when he hit top speed. Can you imagine racing on the high-banks at 140 miles per hour with no roof? Panch started the 1959 Daytona 500 in fourth spot, having finished second in the convertible qualifying race. He finished the 500 in seventeenth place, the second-highest finishing "ragtop." Panch had a leather cover made to cover all but the driver's seat area, enhancing the aerodynamics of the open-topped racer. Midway through the race, the cover came loose and began to whip him in the face. Panch had to finish the race steering with one hand and holding the leather cover down with the other.

The NASCAR Convertible division was dropped after the 1959 season. The ragtops never again raced in the Daytona 500, but the memory of that event will stay with Marvin Panch forever.

Said Panch: "I earned every penny of that $500 bonus."

into the International Motorsports Hall of Fame. And in 1998 he was named one of the "50 Greatest NASCAR Drivers of All Time" by NASCAR.

One of the greatest begat, of course, the driver many consider *the* greatest. And during his career, seven-time champion Dale Earnhardt made a habit of acknowledging his father's talent and legacy. Dale Earnhardt also acknowledged the sadness he felt that his father never lived to see him reach NASCAR's pinnacle. The first of Dale Earnhardt's seven championships came in 1980—seven years after his father's death.

A DREAM MADE FROM DIRT: DAYTONA INTERNATIONAL SPEEDWAY

Today's successes were, at some point, yesterday's dreams.

And make no mistake: Daytona International Speedway was a dream. In fact, even when the dream was coming to fruition for Bill France, there were naysayers about spreading the word that Big Bill was dreaming still.

France, as always, forged on when faced with adversity, proving once again that he was the living, breathing embodiment of one of his favorite sayings.

"On the plains of hesitation lie the bleached bones of countless millions who, when within the grasp of victory, sat and waited—and waiting died."

Make no mistake, Bill France was not in favor of waiting. His determination to craft a 2.5-mile superspeedway from the muck and sand of coastal Florida would become part of NASCAR lore, and part

of its foundation. Read this recent statement by current NASCAR president Mike Helton:

"While NASCAR has taken advantage of opportunities that were presented, there were other times when we created our own opportunities."

Building Daytona International Speedway was all about creation. Big Bill himself spent many an afternoon on a bulldozer, moving and piling the grainy, sandy soil, layer upon layer, building impossible-to-imagine banks at thirty-one-degree angles that would be covered with pavement. The idea was that the

banking would allow cars to maintain extremely high speeds even while cornering.

The project lasted from 1957 to '59, with a couple of financially induced hiccups along the way. As 1959 dawned, Daytona International Speedway awaited the first running of the Daytona 500.

ABOVE: Proud papa Bill France Sr. with his baby, Daytona International Speedway, in 1958.
OPPOSITE: Paving Daytona International Speedway's first turn (1958). It was an unprecedented job, with equipment being designed specifically for this task.

"The beach course had been moved further and further south with the development of Daytona Beach. But even the south peninsula was starting to grow as we got into the 1950s. And

THE CROWDS GREW.

What never changed was the amount of time you had between high tide and low tide. So as the crowds grew, it took longer to get them and longer to get them off the beach."

—BILL FRANCE JR. ON BEACH RACING AND THE NEED
FOR DAYTONA INTERNATIONAL SPEEDWAY[6]

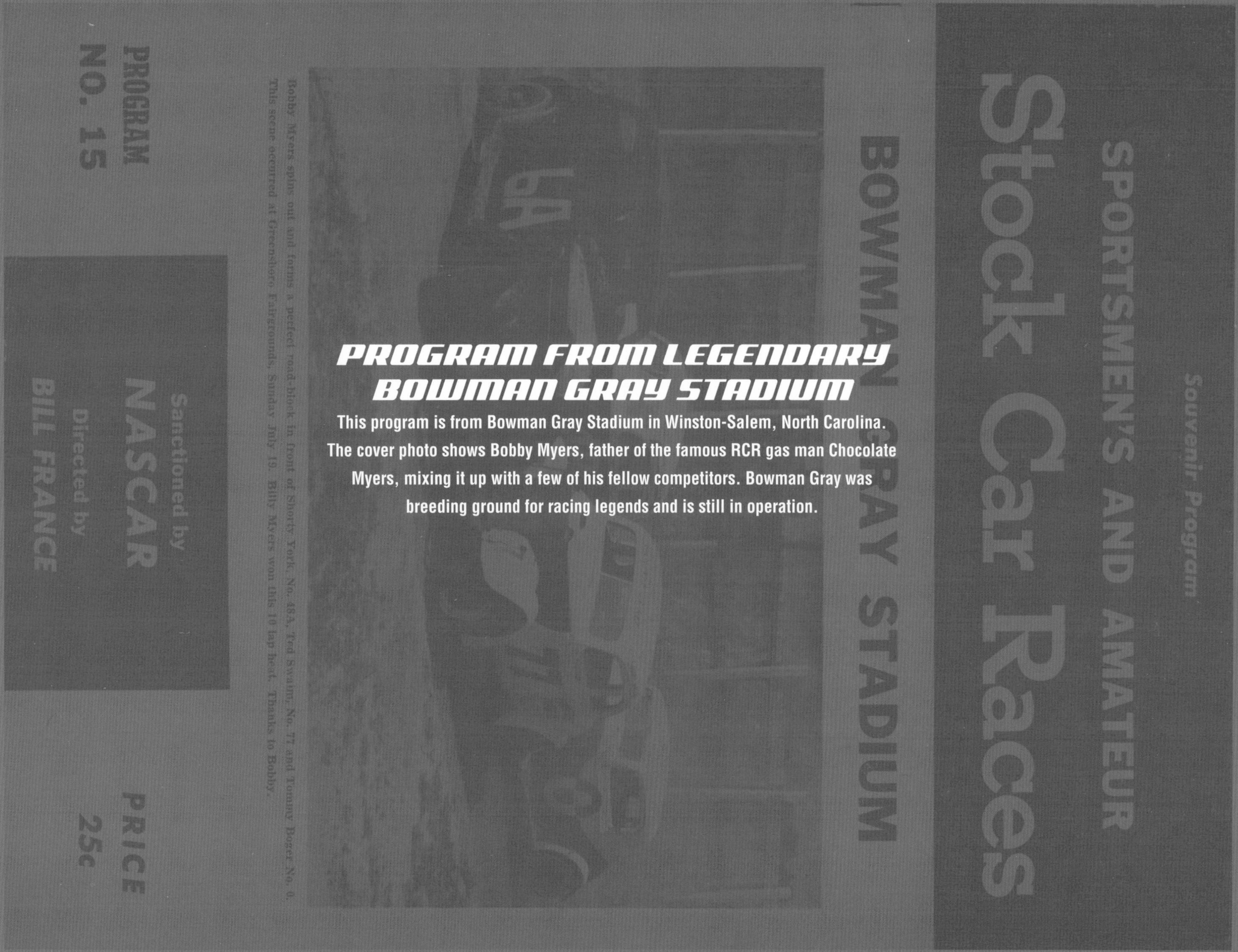

PROGRAM FROM LEGENDARY BOWMAN GRAY STADIUM

This program is from Bowman Gray Stadium in Winston-Salem, North Carolina. The cover photo shows Bobby Myers, father of the famous RCR gas man Chocolate Myers, mixing it up with a few of his fellow competitors. Bowman Gray was breeding ground for racing legends and is still in operation.

Souvenir Program

SPORTSMEN'S AND AMATEUR

Stock Car Races

BOWMAN GRAY STADIUM

PROGRAM NO. 15

Sanctioned by
NASCAR
Directed by
BILL FRANCE

PRICE 25c

Bobby Myers spins out and forms a perfect road-block in front of Shorty York, No. 48A, Ted Swaim, No. 7, and Tommy Pager, No. 0. This scene occurred at Greensboro Fairgrounds, Sunday July 15. Billy Myers won this 10 lap heat. Thanks to Bobby.

ABOVE: The banked turns at Daytona International Speedway made it possible for drivers to corner at high speeds, and earned the track the nickname "Daytona Speed Plant."

OPPOSITE: One of several photos of the dramatic finish that Bill France used to determine the winner of the first Daytona 500.

PETTY CASHES IN AFTER 500 MILES—AND THREE DAYS OF DEBATE

No way could it have been scripted any better: The first Daytona 500. The Debut of Daytona International Speedway. A too-close-to-call finish featuring Lee Petty and Johnny Beauchamp. An all-call by Bill France—to wire services and anyone else possessing adequate shutter speeds—for photographs that would help determine who exactly was the winner.

It took three days.

During that time, NASCAR stayed on the tips of millions of tongues and on the fingertips of thousands of reporters, typing madly on their now-extinct Royal keys—ribbon-ruining typing—trying to explain to readers just what was developing down there in Daytona Beach, Florida. Stock car racing was for the first time flirting with the consciousnesses of sporting fans throughout the nation.

Under normal circumstances, deciphering a photo-finish winner might not have taken three days. But in this instance, the lap-down, No. 73 Chevrolet driven by Joe Weatherly crossed the finish line ahead of Petty's

No. 42 Oldsmobile and Beauchamp's No. 48 Ford, obscuring the view from the flagstand where France was standing alongside the race's flagman.

After studying photos for three days, on the night of Wednesday, February 26, France announced that Petty had won the first Daytona 500.

An interesting footnote: the other Petty in the field, a young, gangly man named Richard, finished fifty-seventh in the fifty-nine-car field. A raw rookie, he joined in the celebration of his father's victory and yearned for the day of his own celebrations.

OPPOSITE: Lee Petty accepts his trophy three days after winning the first Daytona 500.
RIGHT: Iowa's Johnny Beauchamp enjoys the spoils of victory at Daytona after he was initially flagged the winner of the inaugural race.

NASCAR INTERNATIONAL

CHAPTER THREE

1960s

A DECADE OF PERSONALITIES, PEARSON, AND PETTY

L ee Petty's controversial win at Daytona set the stage for yet another successful year for Petty Enterprises. Petty went on to win the 1959 NASCAR Grand National championship, making him the first driver to capture three crowns in NASCAR's premier series.

Petty and the rest of NASCAR's star drivers showed they could make the transition from dusty dirt tracks to the new high-speed raceways with relative ease.

American stock car racing was getting into uncharted territory with the opening of the new "speed plant" known as Daytona International Speedway. No one had experienced those high speeds in the past, and there were several unknown factors to consider: aerodynamics, tire stability, and the overall endurance of engines and chassis. Surprisingly, the 1959 Daytona 500 was run without a single accident or caution period.

The building of the speedway ushered in NASCAR's initial era of superspeedway development. Within eighteen months of Daytona's inaugural event, 1.5-mile speedways were opened in Charlotte, North Carolina, Hanford, California, and Atlanta, Georgia. Before the decade was over, large tracks would be built at Rockingham, North Carolina, and Talladega, Alabama.

Both the Atlanta and Charlotte tracks were high-banked, which made for lightning-fast speeds and lots of action. Both cities had a great auto-racing heritage dating back to the early twentieth century, and these new superspeedways assured them a continued place in racing history.

Atlanta's inaugural race, held on July 31, 1960, was won by the great Fireball Roberts. The race went off without a hitch. However, the same can't be said for Charlotte's

PAGE 66: Paul Goldsmith flashes down the front stretch at Atlanta Raceway in 1966.
LEFT: Edward Glenn "Fireball" Roberts, NASCAR's first superstar.
OPPOSITE: Starter Johnny Bruner Sr. takes a daring stand as he flags off the field for a qualifying race at Daytona International Speedway in July 1960.

"The 1961 Rebel 300 was my biggest win. I caught Curtis Turner with two laps to go and made the pass. I was determined to pass him. He had blocked me for fifteen laps. Ralph Moody had told me all week how to do it. He told me I'd have to make the pass on Turner low going into the turn. How did he know it would be between me and Turner?

RALPH WAS A GENIUS.

He knew things would happen long before they did happen. I learned so much from him. "

—FRED LORENZEN ON THE EARLY DAYS OF HIS CAREER

first event. Speedway construction was held up due to financial problems, and the race, known as the World 600, "racing's longest and most grueling late-model stock car race," was rescheduled from May 20, 1960, to June 19. Paving of the speedway was still under way the morning of first-round qualifying. With no time for the asphalt to cure, the surface quickly broke apart during qualifying and practice. The drivers were instructed to install truck mud flaps across the rears of their cars and to use screening across their windshields and grilles to stop the flying chunks of errant surface. "The cars look more like Army tanks than race cars," quipped Lee Petty.

Jack Smith was leading the race by five laps with only forty-eight laps to go when a piece of asphalt punctured his gas tank. He was forced to the pits for repairs and finished twelfth, while Tennessee's Joe Lee Johnson cruised to the biggest victory of his career.

THE GOLDEN BOY: A NEW BREED OF NASCAR DRIVER

A new breed of driver emerged with the advent of superspeedways: one who used strategy to win a race, a real "thinking" driver who relied on his mind and not just his heavy right foot.

A blond-haired Adonis named Fred Lorenzen was the first such driver. He set the standard for generations of future cerebral chauffeurs. Lorenzen hailed from, of all places, Chicago, where he made a name for himself on the

Program from the first event held at Charlotte Motor Speedway (now Lowe's Motor Speedway), May 1960. Joe Lee Johnson won the race after the track surface broke up, causing a hole in race leader Jack Smith's fuel tank.

THE *First* ANNUAL

WORLD 600

CHARLOTTE MOTOR SPEEDWAY
HOME OF THE "WORLD 600"

OFFICIAL PROGRAM

PRICE 1.oo

NASCAR

RICHARD PETTY

RENE CHARLAND

BOBBY ALLISON

Stock Car Racing Record Book

1965

FOR... PRESS...RADIO
TELEVISION

OFFICIAL SOUVENIR
PROGRAM
$1.00

18th ANNUAL

SOUTHERN 500

Labor Day, Sept. 4, 1967
DARLINGTON RACEWAY

Nº 10290

OPPOSITE LEFT: 1965 NASCAR record book featuring
division champions for the 1964 season.
OPPOSITE RIGHT: Program from the 1967 Southern 500
at Darlington. Richard Petty won the event on his way
to a record-breaking season and his second of seven
NASCAR championships.
BELOW: Program from the 1963 Daytona 500.
RIGHT: Program from the 1962 Daytona 500 and
Speed Weeks. Fireball Roberts dominated the races,
winning every event that he entered.

DAYTONA
INTERNATIONAL
SPEEDWAY

NASCAR
INTERNATIONAL

15th Annual NASCAR Safety & Performance Trials
NASCAR Late Model Championship Stock Car Races
NASCAR Championship Modified - Sportsmen Races

15TH ANNUAL
DAYTONA 500
& DAYTONA SPEED WEEKS
Program No. 3
Feb. 18-24

OFFICIAL SOUVENIR PROGRAM

PURE
BE SURE WITH PURE

PRICE $1.00

Hal Johnson

PRICE $1.00

FOURTH ANNUAL
"DAYTONA 500"
& 1962 DAYTONA SPEED WEEKS

NASCAR Safety & Performance Trials
Model Championship Stock Car Races
mpionship Modified - Sportsmen Races
et Races
Races

NASCAR
INTERNATIONAL

DAYTONA
INTERNATIONAL
SPEEDWAY

The World's Finest and Fastest Speedway

AL SOUVENIR PROGRAM

PURE
BE SURE WITH PURE

Hal Johnson

ABOVE: Fred Lorenzen (No. 28) follows his idol Fireball Roberts during the 1961 Firecracker 250 at Daytona. This photo was taken in front of what later would become the Fireball Roberts Grandstand.

OPPOSITE: "Golden Boy" Fred Lorenzen with his 1963 Holman-Moody-prepared Ford. This team scored the first $100,000 season in NASCAR history.

United States Auto Club (USAC) stock car circuit, winning that series' championship in 1959.

Lorenzen was first noticed by the wily Ralph Moody, of the famed Holman-Moody Ford factory racing team. The "Golden Boy," as Lorenzen came to be known, burst upon the NASCAR scene in 1961 with Moody acting as teacher.

The young pupil immediately put his name in the record books by beating the old pro, Curtis Turner, in a Convertible Division race at Darlington. Turner was so incensed at being beaten by the young pup that he took out his frustration by running into Lorenzen's car on the cool-down lap.

Lorenzen continued to burn up the superspeedways, only occasionally competing on short tracks. He won six races in 1963, and achieved what was thought to be an unattainable goal. Fred Lorenzen won over $100,000 in a single season. To make the feat even more remarkable, he competed in only twenty-nine of the season's fifty-five events. His final tally for race winnings in 1963 was $122,587.

Fred Lorenzen's driving record consists of twenty-six victories in NASCAR's premier series, including the 1965 Daytona 500. He retired from driving in 1972 and went on to a successful career in the Chicago real estate market.

SEVENTH ANNUAL

DAYTONA 500

17th Annual NASCAR Safety and Performance Trials • NASCAR Late Model Championship Stock Car Races • NASCAR Championship Modified - Sportsmen Races • ARCA Late Model Stock Car Races

1965 DAYTONA SPEEDWEEKS - Program No. 1, Feb. 3 - 14

DAYTONA *International* SPEEDWAY
DAYTONA BEACH, FLORIDA
The World's Finest and Fastest Speedway
OFFICIAL SOUVENIR PROGRAM $1.00

HOMETOWN HERO—GLENN (DON'T CALL ME "FIREBALL") ROBERTS

Every sport seems to have a star shining brighter than the rest, whose deeds and accomplishments make a bigger impact, whose name lingers a little longer on the tongue.

Such a star was Glenn "Fireball" Roberts.

Although he's remembered as a Daytona Beach–based driver, Roberts was actually born in Tavares, Florida, in 1929. His family moved to Daytona Beach during Roberts' high school days. He acquired his nickname because of his prowess as a baseball pitcher for an American Legion team, the Apopka Mud Hens. Roberts always hated his colorful nickname, and if you were in his presence you had better call him Glenn.

Roberts also pitched on the University of Florida baseball team while a student in the school's mechanical engineering program in the late 1940s. During this time, Roberts became acquainted with Daytona's favorite race-driving son, the legendary Marshall Teague. Teague quickly became the young athlete's mentor, and Roberts' dream of an engineering degree evaporated as quickly as smoke from a Ford flat-head's exhaust pipe. The racing bug had bitten Glenn Roberts and, as far as he was concerned, there was no cure.

LEFT: Program from the 1965 Daytona 500. The look of the speedway certainly has changed a bit from those days.
OPPOSITE: The immortal Fireball Roberts beside his purple 1963 Ford Galaxie. He won the 1963 Southeastern 500 at Bristol in his first start with a Ford, after driving Pontiacs for the previous four seasons.

ABOVE: Fireball Roberts in his potent 1962 Pontiac, the car that dominated the 1962 Daytona Speed Weeks.
OPPOSITE: Bobby Johns (No. 72) shares a row with Fireball Roberts before the 1962 Firecracker 250 at Daytona International Speedway.

Teague and Roberts hit the NASCAR modified circuit throughout the Southeast, and the pupil showed promise. In 1950 Roberts finished second in the inaugural Southern 500 at Darlington, while only twenty-one years of age. He had scored his first premier-series win at Hillsboro, North Carolina, just a few weeks earlier, making him one of the youngest drivers to win a NASCAR event. Roberts finished the season runner-up in points to series champion Bill Rexford.

It was hard for Roberts to find quality equipment to race in NASCAR's premier series during the next several seasons. So he concentrated on the Modifieds—a division for two-door coupes, predominantly Fords built from 1938 to 1940, running highly modified engines, hence the series' name. Roberts' big break came in 1956 when he was tabbed to drive for Pete DePaolo and the newly formed Ford factory racing team. That year he won six races in the Grand National Division and established himself as a true star, his colorful nickname helping him to become stock car racing's first nationally recognized personality.

Roberts continued to win major events for the next several seasons, including a sweep of all the 1962 events at Daytona. In 1964 an accident on the backstretch at Charlotte Speedway during the World 600 cut Fireball Roberts' life short, but he had made an indelible mark in NASCAR's history book, with thirty-three victories in the premier series.

WHEN KING RICHARD WAS ONLY A PRINCE . . .

Had Richard Petty become anything but a race car driver, most folks would still be scratching their heads. His dad, Lee, was a three-time NASCAR champion with fifty-four wins to his credit. The younger Petty had grown up with race track clay and racecar grease under his fingernails. It was only natural that he would follow in his father's tire tracks.

How odd that one of America's greatest sports heroes, Richard Petty, competed in his first NASCAR race in Canada. The year was 1958. Lee wouldn't let his son race until he turned twenty-one years of age, and coincidentally, the race at Toronto was the first event on the NASCAR schedule after that birthday. By 1964, the year of his first championship, Richard Petty had already

---

OPPOSITE: Donnie Allison, driving Banjo Matthews' Ford, and Richard Petty in the Petty Engineering Plymouth prepare for the start of the 1968 Southern 500 at Darlington Raceway. Note the famed "Darlington stripe" along Petty's right rear fender.
TOP: Richard, Lee, and Maurice Petty share the joy of Richard Petty's first NASCAR championship (1964).
BOTTOM: Richard Petty acknowledges the crowd as he sits atop his Plymouth in Daytona International Speedway's Victory Lane after winning the 1964 Daytona 500. It was the first of Petty's seven Daytona 500 victories.

scored twenty-eight wins and had established himself as a contender.

The 1964 NASCAR Grand National season began on November 10, 1963, at Concord, North Carolina. Petty scored a win at Savannah, Georgia, on December 29, for his initial victory of the season. The first major race of 1964 was the Daytona 500, a race his dad won in '59.

Petty was confident his Hemi-powered Plymouth Fury would show the rest of the field its rear bumper, and he was right: the Petty-Fury combo dominated the race. Richard Petty finished the season with nine wins and forty-three top-ten finishes in sixty-one starts for the first of his seven championships in NASCAR's premier series.

A YEAR NEVER TO BE MATCHED

History was truly made during the 1967 NASCAR season—history that most likely will never be matched. Among the records set by Richard Petty that year were the following:

- Total victories for a season: 27
- Consecutive victories: 10
- Victories from the pole: 15

In addition, Petty ended the year with seventy-five career victories, having smashed his father's previous series record of fifty-four.

TOP: Curtis Turner, wheeling Smokey Yunick's controversial Chevelle, leads the field for the start of the 1967 Daytona 500. Mario Andretti won the event—his only NASCAR victory.
BOTTOM: NASCAR vice president Lin Kuchler presents Richard Petty his second championship trophy (1967).
OPPOSITE: Richard Petty behind the wheel of his electric blue Plymouth, which made a shambles of the competition during NASCAR's 1967 season.

NASCAR SUPERCARS

1960s: Plymouth

• **TOP DRIVER:** Richard Petty

• **OTHER MEMORABLE DRIVERS:**
  Lee Petty, Jim Paschal, Tiny Lund,
  Marvin Panch

• **RACES WON:** 133

• **CHAMPIONSHIPS:**
  Richard Petty in 1964 and 1967

NOTABLE: Richard Petty drove his Hemi-powered Plymouth to a convincing win at the 1964 Daytona 500. It was Petty's first of seven Daytona 500 victories. Marvin Panch won the 1966 World 600 in a year-old Plymouth that Richard Petty used on the dirt tracks. The 1967 Petty Plymouth totally dominated the NASCAR circuit. Richard Petty won twenty-seven races, including a stretch of ten in a row. Petty grabbed 101 of the 133 checkered flags taken by Plymouth drivers in the 1960s.

The 1967 season remains the most successful year enjoyed by any team in NASCAR history in terms of victories. Richard Petty had become "The King." Said NASCAR founder Bill France Sr. toward the end of Petty's career, "I know of no other driver in NASCAR history who brought more recognition to the sport."

Giving praise to his crew after the 1967 title was won, Richard said, "Most of the credit for our success should go to Maurice [his brother], Dale Inman [his cousin], Smoky McCloud, Tom Cox, and Alex Yoder. Oh yeah, don't forget about the Old Man [his father, Lee]. He still has a lot to do with this operation." The year marked Petty's second NASCAR championship.

LITTLE DAVID, THE GIANT KILLER

David Pearson grew up in Whitney, South Carolina—a textile town—with the desire to do more with his life than work in the local mill. He had a penchant for speed, and he seemed to be able to handle a car pretty well. Maybe, just maybe, he thought, he could be a race car driver.

After all, in 1943 he won a wagon race with his pet goat providing the pulling power. Eventually Pearson scraped a few bucks together, bought an old Ford, and went racing.

He was successful enough to get the attention of racing great Joe Littlejohn. Pearson entered big-time NASCAR racing in 1959 and won the 1960 NASCAR Grand National Rookie of the Year title. About that time, master car builder Ray Fox was looking for a driver to wheel his powerful Pontiac in the 1961 World 600 at Charlotte. Littlejohn suggested Pearson. The young dirt-track ace scored a major win in the 600.

"It was May 28, 1961," Pearson recalled. "That's the day I became a full-time race car driver.

"It's the biggest race I ever won and I reckon it always will be, because it was the first big race I won. I kept thinking during the race that I was in a dream or something, because I was outrunning Fireball Roberts and all the others. I never thought about the money I'd get or anything, because I was just so happy I was winning. It was the best feeling in the world when I finally crossed the finish line and they waved the checkered flag. I guess I was as happy right then as I've ever been in my life."

David Pearson found success behind the wheel of Cotton Owens-prepared Dodges from 1962 to '67. Pearson won the 1966 NASCAR championship while driving for Owens.

1963
NASCAR LICENSE

Sam Packard was a founding member of NASCAR in 1947, and he later became a NASCAR inspector. Here is a reproduction of his 1963 NASCAR license.

RACE REPORT
FROM LORENZEN'S
HISTORIC SEASON

In 1963 Fred Lorenzen became the first driver to win over $100,000 in a single NASCAR season. Here is an official NASCAR race report showing one of Lorenzen's victories during that historic season.

1966
CHARLOTTE
SPEEDWAY
PROGRAM

Lowe's Motor Speedway was known as Charlotte Speedway in 1966, and, like today, it offered some of the best races on the NASCAR schedule.

Pearson went on to win two more major events in 1961. This was unheard of for a relative newcomer. Pearson suddenly was dubbed "Little David, the Giant Killer."

Later in his career, after building a reputation as a master tactician on the race track, Pearson picked up another moniker reflecting his cunning style: "The Silver Fox."

After 1961, he continued with some success, racking up thirteen wins through the 1965 season. In 1966 Pearson won the first of his three NASCAR championships driving Cotton Owens' Dodge. The potent pair scored fifteen wins in forty-two starts, all but dominating the season.

Pearson switched rides in 1967, taking up with the Holman-Moody factory-backed team. He won his second championship in 1968, driving a Ford to sixteen victories and thirty-six top-five finishes in forty-seven starts. Again, Little David was slaying giants.

His final title came in 1969, via eleven wins and forty-two top-five finishes in fifty-one starts. Having won three championships during the decade, some would contend that David Pearson was the most successful driver of the 1960s.

With a total of 105 career victories, Pearson is second to Richard Petty on the all-time win list. And despite the fact that Petty has two hundred, the ninety-five-victory gap closes quickly in some conversations when people compare and contrast the two greats.

TOP: David Pearson (No. 6) duels with Darel Dieringer at Asheville, North Carolina, in 1966. It was Pearson's first championship season.

BOTTOM: Young upstart David Pearson (left) runs wheel-to-wheel with defending NASCAR champ Rex White during the 1961 Dixie 400 at Atlanta. Pearson took the win for his third major victory of the year.

"

I kept thinking during the race
that I was in a dream or something, because

I WAS OUTRUNNING FIREBALL ROBERTS AND ALL THE OTHERS.

I never thought about the money I'd get or anything, because I was just so happy I was winning. It was the best feeling in the world when I finally crossed the finish line and they waved the checkered flag. I guess I was as happy right then as I've ever been in my life.

"

—DAVID PEARSON ON HIS 1961 WORLD 600 VICTORY

There is a general acknowledgement that, overall, Petty raced with better equipment over the course of his career. Pearson supporters often point to that when making the argument that he was superior to Petty. There is also the matter of total starts to consider. Petty has the all-time record of 1,185, more than double Pearson's 574.

"Petty fans and Pearson fans will always debate which driver is better," said Jim Hunter, author of *21 Forever: The Story of Stock Car Driver David Pearson*.

"Both groups are understandably biased."

TALLADEGA: ANOTHER DREAM COME TRUE FOR BIG BILL

With the opening of Daytona International Speedway, Big Bill France's lifelong dream of building a race track to rival the legendary Indianapolis Motor Speedway was realized. By the late 1960s, NASCAR was expanding into a big-time, big-track sport, and France was ready for a new challenge.

He now wanted a track that was bigger, better, and faster than his first love, Daytona. France found land in rural Alabama. He explained his new dream

OPPOSITE: The combination of David Pearson and Holman-Moody scored back-to-back championships with Fords in 1968 and '69.
TOP: This is a classic Pearson-Petty battle with action shown here at Macon, Georgia, in 1967. Pearson (No. 17) switched to the Holman-Moody team in mid 1967.
BOTTOM: David Pearson was adept on all track surfaces. He cut his racing teeth on the dirt tracks of South Carolina and won many dirt events on the NASCAR circuit before dirt-track races were eliminated from the schedule in 1970.

ABOVE: The Alabama International Motor Speedway, later known simply as Talladega Superspeedway, takes shape during its 1968 construction. This pile of dirt would become the fastest race track in the world of NASCAR.

OPPOSITE: A portion of Talladega's front stretch grandstand. It's been said the glass-fronted press box swayed a bit whenever the field of forty-three stock cars thundered by.

to Charlie Moneypenny, the retired engineer for the City of Daytona Beach who had designed Daytona International Speedway. Moneypenny came up with a new and improved version of his first creation.

While Daytona had thirty-one-degree banks and three racing lanes, Alabama International Motor Speedway (the official name of the new track—although it would come to be known simply as "Talladega") would have thirty-three-degree banks and four racing lanes. Daytona was 2.5 miles in length, while Talladega would be 2.66.

Ground was broken in 1968, with the speedway set to open in September 1969. Early testing by the drivers proved the new track to be lightning fast. History would soon be made, most certainly history having to do with speed records.

Chrysler Corporation introduced its new Dodge Daytona ultra-aerodynamic model at Talladega's first race. But history-making was stalled when tires began to break apart and the drivers became unsure of how the racing surface would hold up. The speeds were a

"Cannonball Baker [the late NASCAR commissioner] had a saying.

HE SAID, 'WINNERS NEVER QUIT AND QUITTERS NEVER WIN.'

They [PDA members] quit. These boys [the thirty-six who drove in the race] saved the facility and stock car racing. They [PDA] owe their futures to the guys who ran today—if they have a future."

—BILL FRANCE SR. ON THE FIRST TALLADEGA 500[9]

bit higher than expected, and many of the top drivers opined the track to be unsafe.

Earlier in the year, most of the drivers had formed a union, known as the Professional Driver's Association (PDA). Now, because of the perceived danger, the PDA was going to call a driver's strike, boycotting the race and the new track. Bill France, of course, stuck to his guns, maintaining that the track was safe for racing.

To prove the point, France bought a race-ready Ford for one dollar from his old friend John Holman. France took to the track, turning laps in excess of 175 miles per hour—not bad for a fifty-nine-year-old business executive.

Nonetheless, drivers still chose to boycott the event. Bill France said a race would take place, regardless of the PDA's actions. In order to ensure a full field, he allowed cars from the previous day's Grand American event to enter the race.

The first Talladega 500 went off as planned on September 14, 1969. Bobby Isaac, Dick Brooks, and Tiny Lund were the only "name" drivers in the race, which contained twelve Grand National cars. The rest of the thirty-six-car field consisted of Cougars, Mustangs, Firebirds, and Camaros. There was even an AMC Javelin entered. Drivers such as a very young Richard Childress, Indy legend Jim Hurtubise, ARCA stars Ramo Stott and Les Snow, and NASCAR legend Buck Baker also were included in the impromptu field.

The race was won by newcomer Richard Brickhouse, driving Charlie Glotzbach's purple Dodge Daytona (Glotzbach had chosen to strike). Brickhouse entered into the history books and took home $24,550 for his victory.

NASCAR man Sam Packard in 1975.

SAM PACKARD: A NASCAR MAN FROM THE OUTSET

Sam Packard always seemed to be in the right place at the right time.

Born in 1920 in Rhode Island, he began racing motorcycles and speedboats at an early age. He moved to Daytona Beach, Florida, as a teenager and went to work in Bill France Sr.'s gas station on Main Street.

France was active as a driver on the local scene, and Packard helped with the race car. Packard even raced occasionally on the beach, and later divided his time between Daytona and New England, where he became a standout modified driver.

Sam Packard attended the organizational meeting of NASCAR in December 1947, representing New England. He competed in the first NASCAR race on February 15, 1948, and entered four Grand National races from 1951 to '62.

He later owned Yamaha of Daytona, one of the first Yamaha franchises in America.

When Sam Packard died in March 2003, an important chapter in racing history was closed. He was the last surviving member of the group who met that fateful day in December 1947, the day NASCAR was born.

And of course, Bill France had his own victory over the union: Drivers went back to work four days later. The PDA broke up a few months after that.

Here's a little footnote to the Talladega story: Bill France Sr. felt that although the first Talladega 500 had been run, it was not the race he had promised. He addressed the gathered crowd and told them their tickets for that day's event could be turned in for a future race at either Daytona or Talladega, a classic two-for-one deal every race fan dreams of.

True story: tickets from that first Talladega 500 are still being redeemed some thirty-five years later.

OPPOSITE RIGHT AND LEFT: Richard Brickhouse, grimy and tired after entering his name into the record books by winning the inaugural Talladega 500 in 1969.
RIGHT: Program from the first Talladega 500, featuring national champion David Pearson. Dodge's ultra-aerodynamic Daytona, which was introduced at this event, also made the cover.

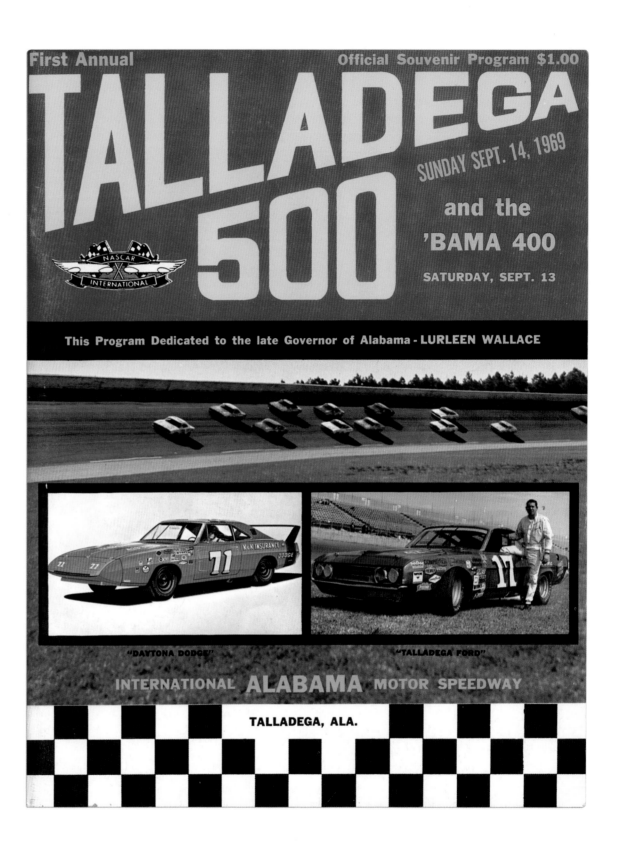

First Annual
Official Souvenir Program $1.00

TALLADEGA 500

and the 'BAMA 400

SUNDAY SEPT. 14, 1969

SATURDAY, SEPT. 13

This Program Dedicated to the late Governor of Alabama - LURLEEN WALLACE

"DAYTONA DODGE"

"TALLADEGA FORD"

INTERNATIONAL ALABAMA MOTOR SPEEDWAY

TALLADEGA, ALA.

CHAPTER FOUR

THE
1970s

A SPORT, APPROPRIATELY, GROWING UP FAST

R. J. Reynolds Tobacco Company had taken notice of NASCAR's rapid growth over the previous several years, and the company concluded that developing a relationship with auto racing would be a great way to showcase its product.

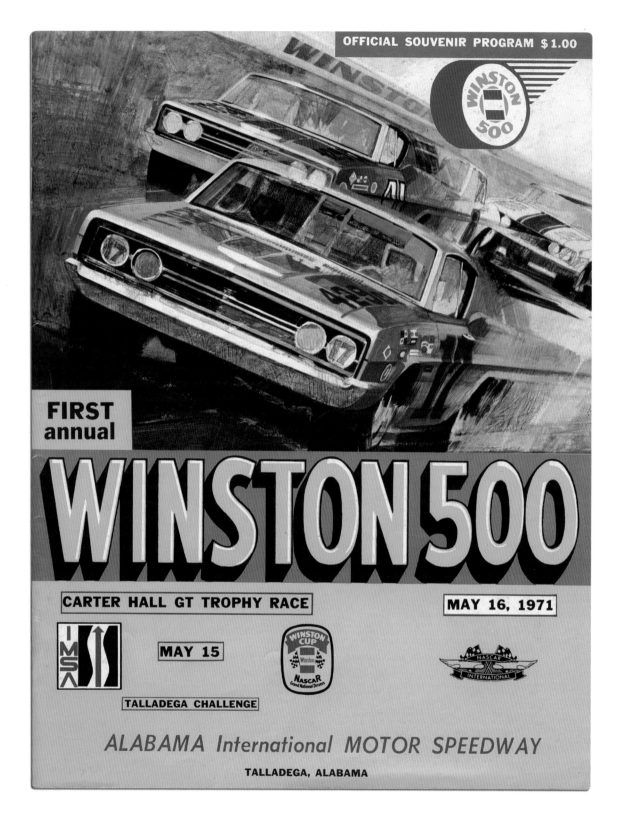

OFFICIAL SOUVENIR PROGRAM $1.00

FIRST annual

WINSTON 500

CARTER HALL GT TROPHY RACE

MAY 16, 1971

MAY 15

TALLADEGA CHALLENGE

ALABAMA International *MOTOR SPEEDWAY*

TALLADEGA, ALABAMA

Reynolds representatives met with NASCAR president Bill France Sr. initially to inquire about sponsorship of a race team. France convinced the group the best way to invest their money was to sponsor the entire series. Heeding France's advice, Reynolds' Winston cigarette brand became the series' title sponsor in 1971.

The game plan for Winston's first season was sponsorship of selected events of 250 miles or longer. These would be known as "NASCAR Winston Cup races." Winston went to great lengths to advertise these races with billboards in areas surrounding the speedways and with advertisements in local newspapers. R.J. Reynolds also introduced a $100,000 bonus that would be shared at the end of the season by the top drivers in the NASCAR point standings.

Donnie Allison has the distinction of winning the first Winston-sponsored race: the 1971 Winston 500 at Talladega.

Winston chose to sponsor the entire Grand National season beginning in 1972. Gone were the one hundred–mile events on short tracks. The 1971 schedule had consisted of forty-eight races with the majority of them being one hundred–milers. In 1972 the schedule was reduced to thirty-one races, but each

PAGE 96: Richard Petty and David Pearson duke it out in a 1973 NASCAR event. These two drivers finished first and second to each other more than any other two drivers in NASCAR history.

LEFT: Program from the 1971 Winston 500, an event that helped to usher in NASCAR's modern era. This was the first race sponsored by Winston. Donnie Allison won in a Wood Brothers Mercury.

OPPOSITE: 1971 Winston 500 winner Donnie Allison is interviewed by legendary announcer Hal Hamrick in Talladega's Victory Lane. The Wood Brothers crew looks on from behind the car.

growth and initial acceptance as a major sport. Big Bill was sixty-two years old when he felt it was time to turn the reins over to the next generation.

His son Bill France Jr., only thirty-eight years old at the time, assumed the duties of the NASCAR presidency on January 11, 1972, when he was handed the keys to the "family business." A new era was ushered in, an era that would see the sport grow beyond everyone's dreams. Everyone, that is, except Bill France Sr.

In 1965 Big Bill said he was certain "NASCAR would be as big as the stick-and-ball sports by the turn of the century." Bill Sr. died in 1992, but had he lived, he would have seen his prophecy come true.

1976 DAYTONA 500: THE BEST FINISH EVER

NASCAR legends Richard Petty and David Pearson had a rivalry for the ages.

The most memorable finish between the two was the 1976 Daytona 500. They waged a torrid duel for most of the race, with Pearson taking the lead eight times and Petty taking the lead on five occasions. Petty led most of Lap 199, with Pearson sliding into the lead on the backstretch. The two cars were side by side entering the third turn as Pearson drifted high. Petty saw an opportunity on the inside and went for it. The two cars—in a flash of Day-Glo red, white, and blue—touched as they exited the fourth turn, just a few hundred yards from the finish line. Both cars spun into the outside wall, with Pearson sliding across the track to the entrance of pit road,

was at least 250 miles in length. That change ushered in what is referred to as the "modern era."

Winston wanted each race to be a major event, and they worked hard with NASCAR to make it so. The NASCAR Winston Cup Series was born. Richard Petty captured the first official Winston Cup championship in 1972. He would win three more before his retirement in 1992. Winston's association with NASCAR came to an end after the 2003 season. It was the most successful sponsorship in the history of motorsports.

HANDING OVER THE KEYS

Bill France Sr. founded NASCAR in 1947 and remained at the helm of the sanctioning body for the next twenty-four years. He nurtured NASCAR through good times and bad: through manufacturers pouting over changes in the rules, a threat of driver unionization from the Teamsters Union in 1961, a driver's strike at Talladega in '69, and an assortment of other headaches and problems. He also guided NASCAR through a time of

"I bounced off the wall and hit him [Petty], and we both spun out. All I was thinking about at the time was getting to the finish line . . . . I know I was asking the crew where Petty was.

I COULDN'T SEE HIM FOR ALL THE SMOKE.

I knew if he got across the finish line first, he'd be the winner. I was just trying to keep my car running and get there first. You know, when you stop and think about it, I was lucky—because Petty's car wouldn't fire back up. It must have been some finish to watch, huh? "

—DAVID PEARSON RECALLS THE FINISH OF THE 1976 DAYTONA 500[10]

PERMATEX 200
WORLD CHAMPIONSHIP
MODIFIED ROAD RACE

PERMATEX
PRESS KIT COVER

The Permatex Corporation was a great supporter of auto racing. The company sponsored Milt Marion's winning effort in the 1936 Daytona stock car race. Early 1970s modified and sportsman races held at Daytona and select other tracks were known as the Permatex 200, Permatex 300, and so on. Here is a press kit cover from the 1974 Daytona Permatex 200 modified race.

DAYTONA INTERNATIONAL SPEEDWAY
DAYTONA BEACH, FLA.
FEBRUARY 15, 1974

Permatex

24 Hours of Daytona®
January 31, - February 1, 1976

1976
SPEEDWEEKS
BROCHURE

The 1976 Daytona 500 featured what has been called racing's most exciting finish. David Pearson and Richard Petty had an incident coming down for the checkered flag. This brochure shows all of the 1976 Daytona Speedweeks events. You can see Daytona International Speedway offered a great schedule of attractions back in our bicentennial year.

ABOVE: Richard Petty leads a six-wide field into the first turn at the start of the 1974 Daytona 450. The Daytona 450? Yes. All NASCAR race distances were cut by 10 percent in 1974 due to America's energy crisis.

OPPOSITE: This sequence shows what has been called "NASCAR's greatest finish," the 1976 Daytona 500. Richard Petty and David Pearson tangled while racing for the checkered flag and both hit the wall. Petty's car stalled, and Pearson limped across the line for the win. The bottom right photo shows Pearson in Victory Lane with his trophy.

where he hit the Chevrolet of Joe Frasson, who was trying to escape the wreckage.

Petty bounced off the outside wall and spun crazily down the track, stopping less than one hundred feet from glory. He could not move because the radiator on his car was pushed back into the fan blade, keeping the engine from turning over.

Pearson, on the other hand, kept his car running and limped across the finish line for his only Daytona

500 victory. Petty scored a second-place finish, despite being penalized because his crew pushed him over the finish line.

A fan poll compiled several years ago judged the finish as the greatest in NASCAR history. It's hard to argue with that assessment.

1979 DAYTONA 500: THE FIGHT

NASCAR and CBS entered into historic a agreement on May 15, 1978. The contract gave CBS exclusive rights for live, flag-to-flag coverage of the Daytona 500 for the following five years. The 1979 Daytona 500 would be the first time "The Great American Race" was broadcast live in its entirety.

The day started rather ominously, with the race delayed due to a rain shower. But once the event got under way, it was one of the best seen in quite a while. Special attention was paid to a brilliant rookie, Dale Earnhardt, as he carved his way to the front of the field on Lap 44.

Several spins punctuated the action as the race progressed under gray and foreboding skies. The race came down to a side-by-side battle between Cale Yarborough and Donnie Allison.

As the pair entered the backstretch on the final lap, Yarborough went to the inside. As Allison tried to block him, they touched and bumped several times, sending the two cars into the third-turn retaining wall. Both cars ground along the wall, finally shooting across the track before coming to rest in the infield, too damaged to continue. While all this action was occurring, Richard

---

OPPOSITE: One lap to go in the 1979 Daytona 500, Donnie Allison leads Cale Yarborough. Less than forty-five seconds later, NASCAR racing would be changed forever as Allison and Yarborough wrecked in the third turn and "the fight" erupted between Bobby Allison and Yarborough.
TOP: Donnie Allison and Yarborough discuss the third turn "shunt."
BOTTOM LEFT AND RIGHT: Bobby Allison gets involved and tempers flare as track personnel try to break it up.

Petty barely beat Darrell Waltrip to the finish line for his sixth Daytona 500 win.

As Petty celebrated in Victory Lane, Bobby Allison stopped by the third turn accident scene to check on the condition of his younger brother. The older Allison and Yarborough got into a heated argument. Suddenly, fists were flying, punches were thrown, and the drivers fell to the ground. Track attendants jumped into the fray and separated the three, but history had been made.

A national TV audience sat transfixed by the human drama being played out before them. The race broadcast had received a larger-than-usual audience because a huge blizzard had covered most of the Northeast. No other major sporting events were on TV that day, and the weather outside was miserable, causing much of the country to remain housebound. Those factors led many who were not racing fans to tune in. The drama of the finish made many of those viewers into new—and permanent—fans.

The broadcast drew an audience of more than sixteen million and a 10.5 rating. The rating for the last half hour of the show shot to 13.5. By contrast, a golf tournament on another major network received a rating of only 5.5.

This single race has been called the turning point for NASCAR becoming a "national" sport. NASCAR began to grow almost immediately after this race, and it continues to grow to this day, thanks, in large part, to network TV coverage.

OPPOSITE: The STP-Petty crew rides to Victory Lane as Richard Petty earns an unexpected win in the 1979 Daytona 500.
TOP: As part of the festivities, NASCAR stock cars lined up on the White House Ellipse with the Washington Monument as backdrop.

NASCAR GOES TO THE WHITE HOUSE

Former president Jimmy Carter is a longtime NASCAR fan. In 1959 he attended the first Daytona 500. As governor of Georgia, he often saw races at Atlanta Motor Speedway, and he did not forget NASCAR when he reached the White House.

Richard Nixon was the first president to invite representatives of auto racing to the White House, in 1971. NASCAR was a part of those festivities, but not exclusive to the event. Finally, in 1978, with Carter in office, NASCAR was front and center, honored with its own White House gala. The world press focused its attention on the event. As it turned out, President Carter was not able to attend. He was working with Anwar Sadat and Menachem Begin at Camp David as they hammered out a Mideast peace treaty.

First Lady Rosalynn Carter took over as host of the affair, and country music legend Willie Nelson provided the entertainment. All in all, it was a great event. NASCAR had officially arrived.

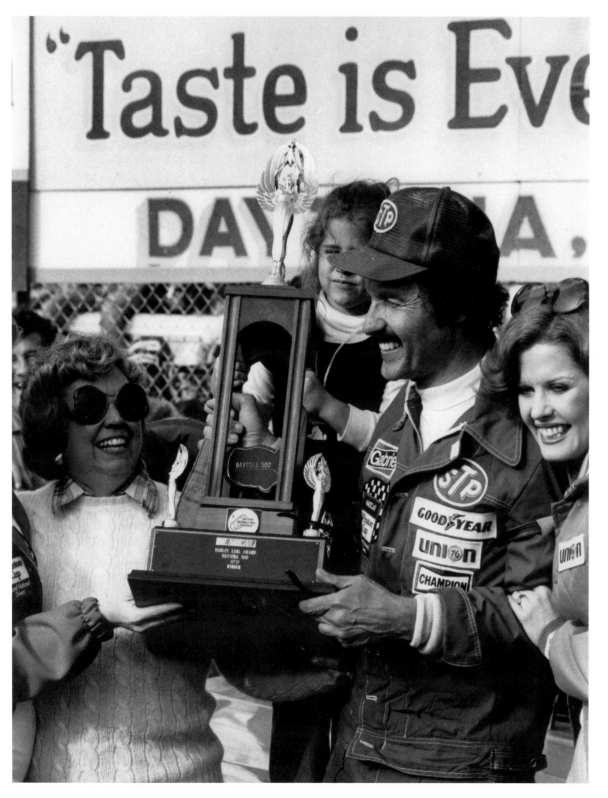

CAMERAS PUT YOU IN THE DRIVER'S SEAT

In the early years of NASCAR, attempts to put a camera inside the driver's compartment of a race car resulted in lackluster imagery, to say the least. Vibration of the race car made for a terrible picture most of the time. The bottom line was that viewers were unable to get a real sense of being in the car with the driver—the technology just wasn't advanced enough to make the camera concept a success.

New camera and mounting technology, however, was developed, and was tried for the first time during the CBS broadcast of the 1979 Daytona 500. Richard Petty and Benny Parsons carried the new, state-of-the-art equipment inside their cars, and it worked like a charm. The cameras were able to rotate and pick up all the action around the cars.

Cale Yarborough became a big proponent of in-car cameras. It seemed every time Yarborough carried a camera in his car at Daytona, he won the race. He thought it to be a good luck charm.

In-car camera technology continues to improve year after year, with equipment becoming smaller and lighter. In-car cameras were an instant hit and have been a major part of all races since that 1979 event.

LEFT: Richard Petty and his wife, Lynda, celebrate Petty's unprecedented sixth Daytona 500 victory (1979).
OPPOSITE: Cale Yarborough grins because he has his good luck charm on board his 1984 Chevrolet: a cumbersome CBS in-car camera. Yarborough seemed to win at Daytona every time he carried a camera into battle.

14TH Annual REBEL 400 salutes
South Carolina's
TRICENTENNIAL

1670 1970
SOUTH CAROLINA
TRICENTENNIAL

TRICENTENNIAL
Edition $1

REBEL
400

N° 3496

SATURDAY, MAY 9, 1970
DARLINGTON RACEWAY
NEXT RACE: *SOUTHERN 500* ~ LABOR DAY, 12 NOON, SEPT. 7, 19

Programs from the 1970 and '71 Rebel 400 at Darlington. The 1970 race was won by David Pearson, fresh off back-to-back NASCAR championships. In 1971 Buddy Baker, driving a Petty Enterprises Dodge, won by a margin of seven laps.

15th Annual
Rebel 400
Sunday, May 2, 1971
A NASCAR Winston Cup Championship Race

REBEL
400

DARLINGTON RACEWAY
Next Race Southern 500 Labor Day, 12 Noon, Sept. 6, 1971
Official Souvenir Program $1.00

TWELFTH ANNUAL
DAYTONA 500

FEBRUARY 22, 1970   12:30 P.M.

WORLD'S FASTEST 500 MILE RACE - WORLD'S FINEST SPEEDWAY

1970 DAYTONA SPEEDWEEKS OFFICIAL SOUVENIR PROGRAM
No. 2   PRICE $2.00

INTERNATIONAL SEDANS SAT., FEB. 7 - 3:30 P.M.	**TWO 125 MILE NASCAR GRAND NATIONAL RACES** THUR., FEB. 19 - 1:00 P.M.
FORMULA VEES SUN., FEB. 8 - 3:00 P.M.	
ARCA 300 MILE RACE SUN., FEB. 15 - 12:30 P.M.	**FLORIDA CITRUS 250** FRI., FEB. 20 - 1:00 P.M.
FORMULA FORD SPECIAL SUN., FEB. 15 - 3:00 P.M.	**DAYTONA PERMATEX 300** SAT., FEB. 21 - 1:00 P.M.

DAYTONA INTERNATIONAL SPEEDWAY

DAYTONA BEACH, FLA.

ABOVE: Program from the 1970 Daytona 500. New Englander Pete Hamilton rocked the racing world by winning not only this race, but also both Talladega events. He drove the beautiful Petty Enterprises Plymouth Superbird to all three wins.

RIGHT: Program from the 1974 Daytona 500. This occurred in the midst of the country's energy crisis, and all NASCAR events were cut by 10 percent. The cover should perhaps have read "The Daytona 450."

RICHARD PETTY

Winner 1973 Daytona 500

Sixteenth Annual

DAYTONA
500

February 17

OFFICIAL SOUVENIR PROGRAM $2.00

DAYTONA SPEEDWEEKS, FEB. 8-17, 1974

☆ ☆ ☆

11th Annual ARCA 200, Feb. 10

☆ ☆ ☆

Two 125 Mile Grand Nationals,
Feb. 14

☆ ☆ ☆

International Race of
Champions, Feb. 15

☆ ☆ ☆

Permatex Modified 200, Feb. 15

☆ ☆ ☆

Daytona-Permatex Sportsman
300, Feb. 16

DAYTONA BEACH, FLORIDA

BENNY PARSONS

1973 Winston Cup Grand National Champion

NASCAR SUPERCARS

1970s: Mercury

- **TOP DRIVER:** David Pearson

- **OTHER MEMORABLE DRIVERS:**
  A.J. Foyt, Donnie Allison,
  Cale Yarborough, Neil Bonnett

- **RACES WON:** 54

- **CHAMPIONSHIPS:**
  None

NOTABLE: The Wood Brothers experienced phenomenal success during the 1970s even though the team competed on a limited schedule, the reason a series championship was never won. David Pearson, who had forty-three victories in the Woods' Mercurys, won eleven consecutive poles at Charlotte and won three races in a row at Darlington.

OL' DW AND THE INTIMIDATOR MAKE THE SCENE

The 1970s produced two of NASCAR's biggest and most controversial stars: Darrell Waltrip and Dale Earnhardt. They were controversial for different reasons: Waltrip seemed to shoot his mouth off so often, he earned the nickname "Jaws." Earnhardt, on the other hand, was a man of few words who let his driving do the talking. He was known for his aggressive bump-and-run style, no doubt learned from his equally aggressive father, Ralph.

Darrell Waltrip competed in his first race in 1972 at Talladega. He drove the same car that carried Mario Andretti to his only NASCAR victory, the 1967 Daytona 500. Waltrip started the race in twenty-fifth position and finished thirty-eighth after his engine blew on Lap 69. Although Waltrip did not capture the Rookie of the Year Award in his first full season of 1973, he went on to win three championships in the '80s.

Dale Earnhardt began his career in NASCAR's premier series at Charlotte Motor Speedway on May 25, 1975, driving Ed Negre's Dodge in the World 600. Ironically, the car carried the number 8, the same number Dale's father, Ralph, made famous on Carolina short tracks. Earnhardt started the race in thirty-third

OPPOSITE: A. J. Foyt scored seven NASCAR wins during his career. Many of those victories came behind the wheel of a Wood Brothers car. Here, Foyt motors to a win in the 1972 Daytona 500.
RIGHT: The 1972 NASCAR season was the first under Winston sponsorship. This program comes from the 1972 Winston 500. David Pearson won the race, and Darrell Waltrip made his first big-league start.

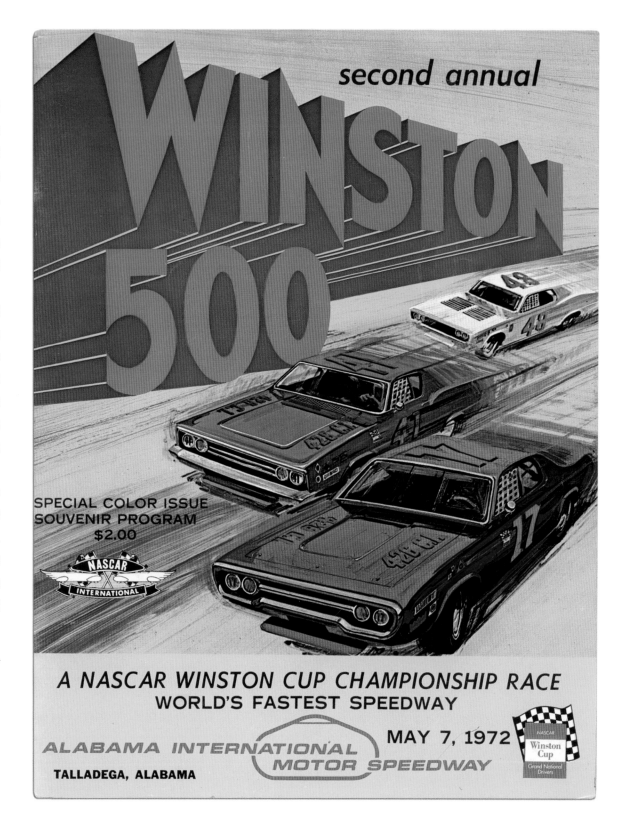

and finished twenty-second, forty-five laps behind race winner Richard Petty.

It was an inauspicious beginning to an eventually storied career. Four years later, Earnhardt won the Rookie of the Year title; a year after that he won the series title. No other driver has won those titles in consecutive years.

Earnhardt claimed seven championships during his career, tying the record set by Richard Petty.

Darrell Waltrip holds the record for most premier series wins in the modern era (1972–present) with eighty-four. He also has the most poles in the modern era: fifty-nine. Waltrip was one of the shrewdest drivers of his time, using strategy to outsmart many of his fellow competitors. He was polished and well spoken—traits that would lead to a broadcasting career after his retirement from driving.

Waltrip and Earnhardt helped spread the "gospel" of NASCAR throughout the sport's modern era. They assisted the sport's transition from each race being, primarily, an event to be witnessed in person, to each race becoming a media event. Waltrip and Earnhardt also became role models for many of today's stars, and both honed the image of today's driver being a media-savvy personality: Waltrip was the first NASCAR driver to host a TV show. Earnhardt was the first to ring the opening bell on the New York Stock Exchange. Each transcended the sport in his own inimitable fashion.

A young, pensive Dale Earnhardt readies himself for the start of his first NASCAR premier series event (1975).

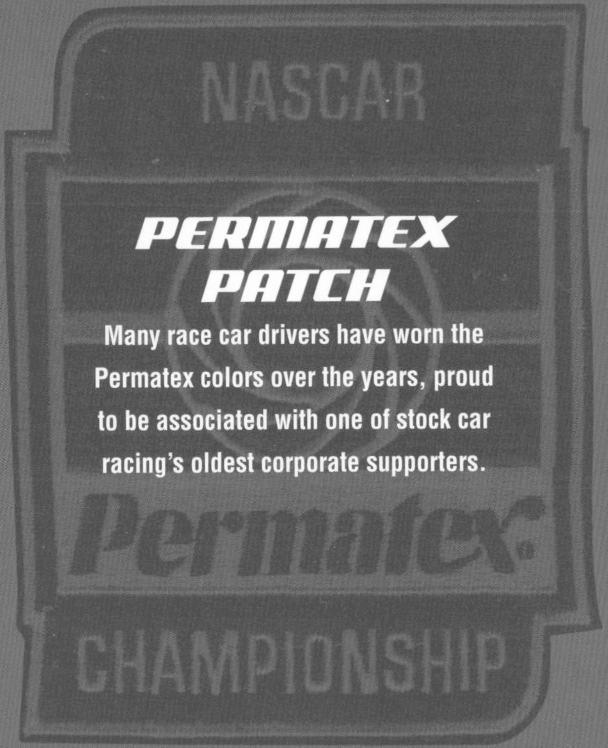

PERMATEX PATCH

Many race car drivers have worn the Permatex colors over the years, proud to be associated with one of stock car racing's oldest corporate supporters.

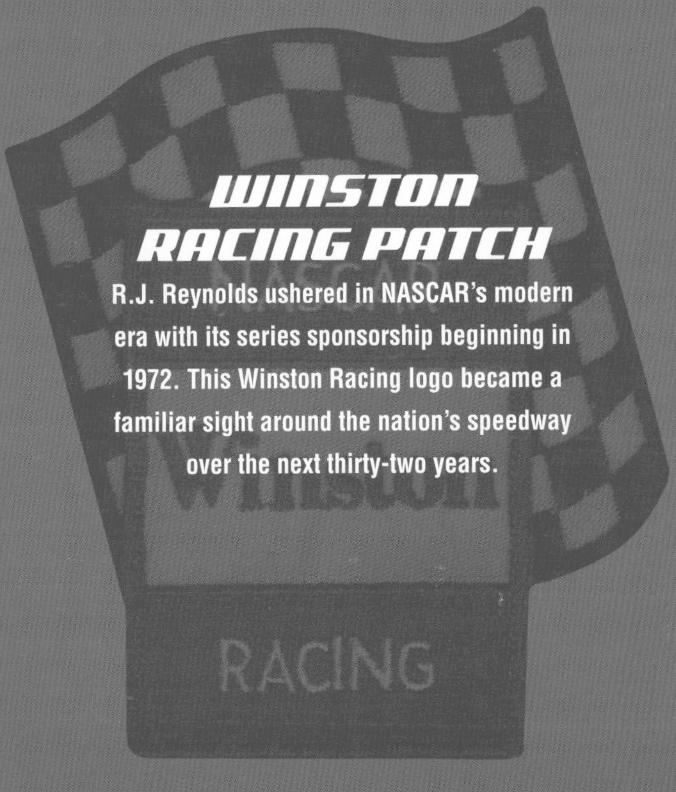

AN INVITATION TO THE WHITE HOUSE

This is the invitation that President Jimmy Carter sent out for his 1978 White House event saluting NASCAR racing. Carter is an old fan of stock car racing dating back to his early days in Plains, Georgia. He supported NASCAR racing during his tenure as the governor of Georgia.

THE PRESIDENT AND MRS. CARTER

welcome NASCAR to

THE WHITE HOUSE

September 13, 1978

WINSTON RACING PATCH

R.J. Reynolds ushered in NASCAR's modern era with its series sponsorship beginning in 1972. This Winston Racing logo became a familiar sight around the nation's speedway over the next thirty-two years.

There are other men who along the way contributed greatly to the evolution of the image of NASCAR drivers as superstars. Fireball Roberts became the sport's first household name, in the 1960s. Richard Petty picked up the baton and ran with it in the 1970s, becoming the sport's first nationally recognized face. Like those two superstars, Darrell Waltrip and Dale Earnhardt were the right men for the right time.

CALE'S THREE-PEAT

Cale Yarborough came to NASCAR with the fiery determination of a bulldog. A stocky fireplug of a man, he had played semipro football before taking up racing for a living. He was known for his tenacity behind the wheel. You could not wear him out. He gained much success driving the beautiful white-and-red No. 21 car for the famed Wood Brothers. Ready for a new challenge, Yarborough moved over to Indy Car racing in the early 1970s.

After a few seasons in the open-wheeled cars, Yarborough realized his true love was stock car racing. Many thought he had burned bridges by leaving NASCAR, and his return was a difficult proposition. He floundered with second-rate equipment for a time before teaming up with Junior Johnson for the 1973

TOP: Richard Petty exits his Plymouth in Victory Lane while announcer Chris Economaki waits for an interview. Petty had just captured the 1973 Daytona 500 after his only competition, Buddy Baker's Dodge, blew an engine with just six laps to go.
BOTTOM: Cale Yarborough won three straight NASCAR championships in the 1970s while driving for Junior Johnson. However, Yarborough gained early success driving for the famed Wood Brothers, shown here in 1968.

" One thing my mom and dad taught me is you had to work hard, so I gauge people by their work ethic. That's one thing I always admired about Earnhardt. **HE WAS A HARD WORKER,** and he instilled that in his kids. **"**

—DARRELL WALTRIP ON DALE EARNHARDT[11]

season. Yarborough quickly got back into the race-winning groove, scoring four wins and finishing second in points in his first full season back in NASCAR.

For all his success, the series championship eluded Yarborough for many years. He finally scored his first in 1976. He had nine wins and twenty-two top-five finishes in thirty starts, beating Richard Petty by a margin of ninety-five points. To back up this feat, Yarborough was champion once more in 1977. Again he won nine times, and again Petty was the points runner-up.

Several drivers had won back-to-back championships, but no one had ever taken three in a row. Cale Yarborough did just that in 1978. From 1976 to '78, Yarborough won nearly a third of the races held. To this day, Cale Yarborough remains the only driver to win three consecutive titles in NASCAR's premier series.

OPPOSITE: Cale Yarborough celebrates a win at Daytona. Note the fairly vacant Victory Lane and compare it to the elaborate and crowded celebrations of today.
RIGHT: Program from the 1976 Daytona 500, called the greatest finish of all time.
PAGE 120: Benny Parsons (No. 27) and Darrell Waltrip (No. 88) lead a pack of cars across the line at Daytona in 1979. Note the dark surface of the newly repaved speedway.

18TH ANNUAL

DAYTONA 500

FEBRUARY 15, 1976

TWO 125-MILE QUALIFYING RACES
FOR DAYTONA 500
Thursday, Feb. 12 — 1:00 p.m.

INTERNATIONAL RACE OF CHAMPIONS
Friday, Feb. 13 — 11:00 a.m.

PERMATEX MODIFIED 200
Friday, Feb. 13 — 1:00 p.m.

DAYTONA PERMATEX 300
Late Model Sportsman
Saturday, Feb. 14 — 1:00 p.m.

1976 Daytona Speedweeks
Souvenir Program and Record Book #2
Feb. 9-15, 1976
Special Issue
Price $3.00

DAYTONA INTERNATIONAL SPEEDWAY
DAYTONA BEACH, FLA. U.S.A.

"We had a successful season, but we had a lot of help. The best team in racing made it possible for me to be here tonight. My primary goal in 1978 was the same as it's always been and the same as it'll always be—to try to do better each year than I did the year before . . .

RACING IS A TOUGH SPORT

and a tough grind. Thank you very much, and I hope I can be right back here again next year. "

—CALE YARBOROUGH ON ACCEPTING THE
1978 NMPA DRIVER OF THE YEAR AWARD[12]

CHAPTER FIVE

THE 1980s

A SHARP TURN TOWARD EXPONENTIAL GROWTH

Came the 1980s and the rumblings were evident. All you had to do was look and listen. NASCAR was seemingly on the cusp of, well, something. At first it was unclear just what exactly that something would turn out to be.

But there was developing gradually and in some corners grudgingly, a conceptual consensus: whatever the future held, it was going to be huge.

The broadcast of the 1979 Daytona 500 had provided a peek at potential, a glimpse of a time soon to come, a time when more than 100,000 fans in the grandstands would always be complemented by millions more watching at home on television.

Emerging was a standard-bearer for NASCAR's future, a driver linked to the sport's past. Dale Earnhardt, an overgrown kid from Kannapolis, North Carolina, son of rough-and-tumble Ralph Earnhardt, won the series championship in 1980. Through the balance of the decade, he would share the spotlight with other future Hall of Fame drivers Darrell Waltrip, Bobby Allison, Bill Elliott, and Rusty Wallace. Those five would account for nine championships in the 1980s, with Earnhardt and Waltrip winning three apiece.

Such a talent combine was timely for NASCAR, because it was essential to make up for Richard Petty no longer being competitive. Petty won his last series championship in 1979. The King, finally, was without a crown.

PAGE 122: The Pontiac Firebird pace car leads a field of forty-two thundering stock cars on a pace lap for the 1983 Daytona 500. Ricky Rudd is on the pole in Richard Childress' Chevrolet. Geoff Bodine flanks him in Cliff Stewart's Gatorade-sponsored Pontiac. Cale Yarborough edged out Bill Elliott by five car lengths for the win.

LEFT: Darrell Waltrip is on his way to winning the 1989 Daytona 500 as he leads Dale Earnhardt, Geoff Bodine, and Phil Parsons. The cars of multicar team owner Rick Hendrick finished first, second, and fourth.

OPPOSITE: The green flag drops on the 1989 Daytona 500 with pole winner Ken Schrader setting the pace. Teammate and race winner Darrell Waltrip starts on the outside in No. 17. Schrader would finish in the runner-up spot this day.

Petty's exit from contention, combining with the championships of Earnhardt and the others, signaled an undeniable changing of the guard. That was apparent.

What was even more apparent was the shifting NASCAR wind, taking a sport up, up, and beyond the confines of its stereotypical Southern past.

Next stop: New York City.

NEW YORK IS INTRODUCED TO A NASCAR STATE OF MIND

Suffice it to say that NASCAR had outgrown the way it honored the champion of its premier series. The former method, a banquet held during February's Speed Weeks leading up to the Daytona 500, had come to seem hurried.

No less than Richard Petty remembers it that way.

"You weren't thinking about the year before," Petty said. "You were thinking about the Daytona 500 that was coming up. It was hard to get into the mind-set of banquet time, because it was racing time."

Bill France, by this time ten years into the job of replacing his father, Bill Sr., as NASCAR's president, applied a broad brushstroke to the NASCAR landscape, one that to this day shapes the sport and how it is viewed on a national level. France decided to take his increasingly big-time sport to an undeniably big-time

RIGHT: "The King" at rest. Richard Petty has been the unofficial ambassador of NASCAR for decades.
OPPOSITE: Darrell Waltrip accepts one of his many awards during NASCAR's first awards banquet at New York City's Waldorf=Astoria Hotel in 1981.

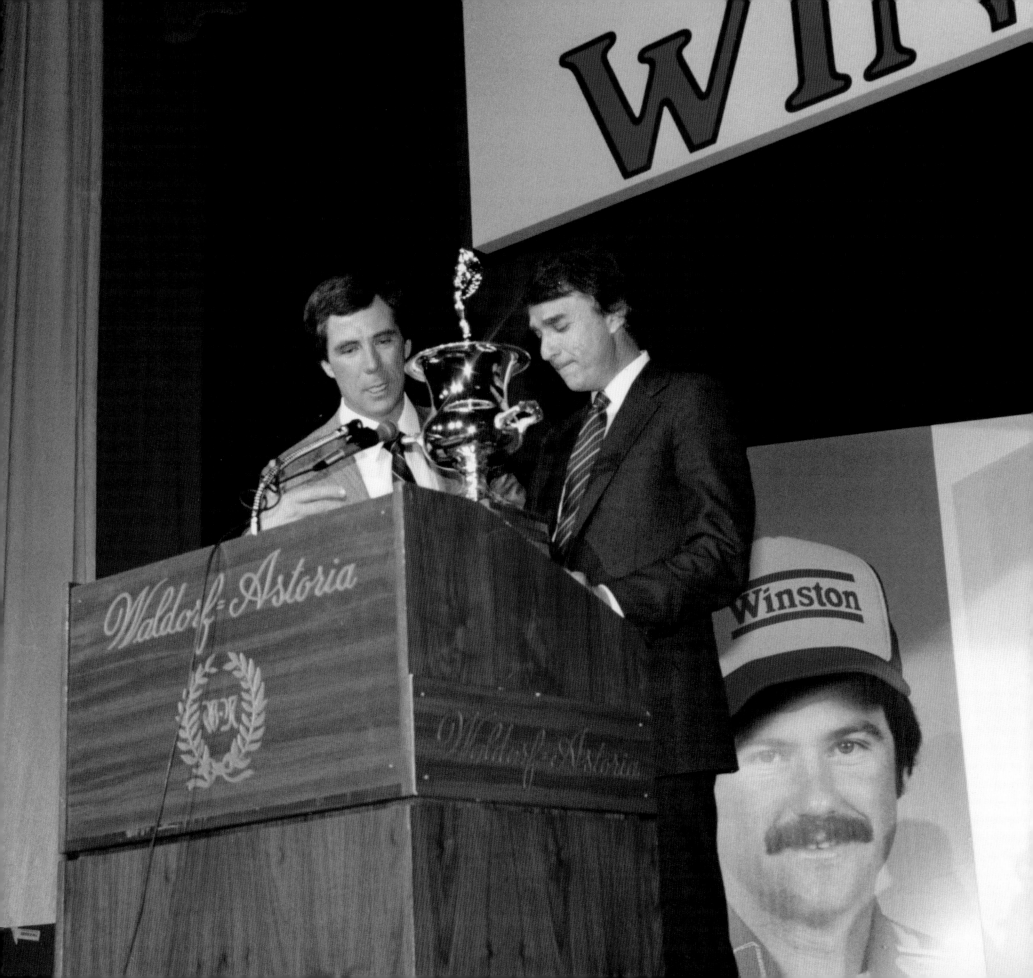

city—New York—and made the banquet a postseason affair. As a kicker, it was arranged for the legendary Waldorf=Astoria Hotel to play host.

Suddenly, in contrast to past years, it was *easy* to get into a banquet frame of mind.

The first champion of NASCAR's premier series to be feted at the Waldorf was Darrell Waltrip, who in 1981 won the first of his three championships in his first year of driving for the already legendary Junior Johnson, a NASCAR mainstay, who had made the transition from pioneer driver to championship car owner.

Waltrip's No. 11 was sponsored by Mountain Dew, hence the nickname for his pit crew, the "Dew Crew."

Waltrip, aided greatly by his crew, overcame a huge midseason deficit to catch Bobby Allison and claim the series championship. Pepsi rewarded the crew by including them in the trip to New York and the championship celebration. NASCAR cooperated graciously by ensuring that the crew workers had seats at the black tie awards banquet.

The men who had toiled all year long, dressed in uniforms adorned with the name of a soft drink, were able to toast their title with glasses of champagne with their driver in the heart of Manhattan.

In the process, they started a tradition. Every year since, the champion's crew has been involved in the "Champion's Week" experience in New York.

TOP: Team owner Junior Johnson (left) and driver Darrell Waltrip (right) formed a potent team that scored two consecutive NASCAR championships in 1981 and '82. They also won the title in 1985.
BOTTOM: Darrell Waltrip inspects work being done under the hood of his Mountain Dew Buick at Martinsville Speedway in 1981.

" The people who have brought this sport where it is have done a hell of a job. We've been competing against sports that have been in existence over one hundred years.

WE'VE COME A LONG WAY IN THIRTY YEARS.

But we have a long way to go. Either we have not had the opportunity to do things off the track, or we haven't made ourselves available. There are some intelligent, class people in NASCAR. We can hold our own against anybody. NASCAR is where it [racing] is. I said that five years ago and people told me to shut up. We're on the edge of doing something big. We've got to get going. **"**

—DARRELL WALTRIP ON NASCAR MOVING ITS AWARDS BANQUET TO NEW YORK CITY, AND THE POSSIBILITIES FOR NASCAR BECOMING A MAINSTREAM SPORT[13]

ROLLING BILLBOARDS: CORPORATIONS START RUNNING FULL-THROTTLE

In the 1980s, NASCAR demographics were speaking to corporate America more than ever before. Or perhaps it's more accurate to say that for the first time, corporate America was listening.

It was likely a combination of both, accented by the ever increasing volume of the NASCAR advertising message, a message prominently scrawled on the corporate consciousness in 1971 when R.J. Reynolds Co. began sponsorship of NASCAR's Grand National Division, which eventually became known as the now-legendary NASCAR Winston Cup Series, which evolved into the NASCAR Nextel Cup Series in 2004.

The Winston brand soon became a weekly demonstration of how NASCAR could help market a product that wasn't automotive-related. The possibilities beyond the auto industry waited in the wings.

By the mid 1980s the gender lines making up the NASCAR fan base had been drawn, with an approximate 60/40 percent male/female split that remains intact to this day. That was a powerful statistic then and still is now.

Back then, the 40 percent female number was an eye-opener—and then, a wallet-opener. It helped

---

OPPOSITE: The team of Dale Earnhardt and Richard Childress dominated the last half of the 1980s. Here, Earnhardt is shown with his 1987 title-winning Chevrolet.
RIGHT: Donnie Allison celebrates in Talladega's Victory Lane after winning the 1977 Talladega 500. Miss Winston, Patti Huffman, later became Mrs. Kyle Petty.

Tide

RACING TEAM

NET WT. 56,000 OZ. (3500 LB.)

lead to a wave of new corporate involvement in NASCAR during the latter half of the 1980s, with teams sponsored by products that were being bought across America mainly by women, products such as Tide Detergent, Folger's Coffee, Crisco Cooking Oil, Bullseye Barbeque Sauce, Heinz Ketchup, Red Baron Pizza, Lifebuoy Deodorant Soap, Slender-U Salons, Under-alls, Country Time Lemonade, and Banquet Foods. Those sponsorships sometimes led to paint schemes that turned race cars into 190 mile-per-hour rolling billboards. The "Tide Machine," originally driven by Darrell Waltrip, was painted just like the detergent box. Bobby Allison's Miller High Life car looked like a giant, gold beer can. The "Folger's Coffee Machine"–driven by Benny Parsons, Ken Schrader, and the late Tim Richmond–wore the same bright red as a packaged pound of coffee.

It was a wondrous, creative time for marketing and NASCAR. For instance, Procter & Gamble came up with the all-time creative media kit to hype the Tide Machine, a folder that looked exactly like the front of a large box of Tide. In the bottom right-hand corner of the kit were numbers listing the size and weight of contents, just like on a detergent box. However, instead of "16 OZ.," you found "56,000 OZ." (the weight of a race car).

As the dollars rolled in, things started moving just as fast off the track. Companies were capitalizing on business-to-business marketing; in hospitality

---

An early Tide Racing Team press kit. Note the imaginative wording: "Winston Cup Size," and also, "NET WT. 56,000 oz. (3500 LB.)," the weight of a NASCAR Winston Cup car.

PROGRAM FROM FIRST NEW YORK AWARDS BANQUET

The amazing growth and exposure of the sport caused NASCAR to move its banquet to the "Big Apple" in 1981. The banquet was held at the famous Waldorf=Astoria Hotel—a perfect, high profile match for NASCAR as they began an era that would see stock car racing compete with other major sports for national attention.

1981

NASCAR Winston-Cup Awards Banquet

OPPOSITE: Darrell Waltrip's crew services the Rick
Hendrick-owned Tide Chevrolet during the 1989 Daytona 500.
TOP: Bobby Allison, followed by his son Davey, roars off the
fourth turn during the 1988 Daytona 500. Father and son
finished first and second, respectively.
BOTTOM: Bobby Allison (center) had a successful NASCAR
career, which included the 1983 NASCAR championship, three
Daytona 500 wins, and eighty-four Winston Cup victories—
tied with Darrell Waltrip for fourth on the all-time win list.

suites, clients were wined, dined, and sold. Meanwhile, a compelling stock car drama played out right in front of them at breathtaking speeds.

The marriage between corporate America and NASCAR had been consummated.

AWESOME BILL AND THE FORD THUNDERBIRD: A MATCH MADE IN AERODYNAMIC HEAVEN

NASCAR is a sport defined by man and machine. At certain junctures in NASCAR's history, defining moments have involved simultaneously a particular man and a particular machine.

Such a moment occurred in the early 1980s when a young, gangly redhead from rural Georgia emerged behind the wheel of unproven, radical-looking, red-gold-and-white Ford Thunderbirds.

Bill Elliott was the driver, and his cars had present and future implications. Space-age in appearance were the new Thunderbirds that first arrived in 1983, with rounded lines that were at the forefront of an aerodynamic revolution affecting both race tracks and showrooms.

Clearly, something special was transpiring.

"Those new T-Birds were downsized; we called the car 'the football' because it was more rounded than anything else out there," said Gary Nelson, NASCAR's managing director of research and development, who was a top crew chief in the 1980s.

At the outset of the 1980s, teams were just beginning to devote an increasing amount of time,

money, and manpower to aerodynamics.

"Then Bill Elliott showed up," Nelson said.

NASCAR was never the same.

"That was a car that was sort of on the cutting edge," said Elliott, downplaying a monumental period as only he could.

"I think back then I was just so involved in the business side and trying to run well, I never really thought about [the T-Bird's technological implications]."

NASCAR was chasing the speed-driven image

of the Indianapolis 500 at the time, recalled Jeff Hammond, Darrell Waltrip's crew chief in the 1980s.

"[The high speeds] kind of put Indy in an elite class," Hammond said. "We at NASCAR were trying to figure out how we could get our cars to go that quick. We wanted to make sure we didn't get left, basically, in the

ABOVE: Bill Elliott is congratulated by his crew after winning the 1987 Daytona 500. Elliott holds the all-time qualifying speeds for Daytona and Talladega.
OPPOSITE: "Awesome Bill from Dawsonville," Bill Elliott, dominated the superspeedways from 1985 through 1987.

"We were quicker when we ran tests here in the winter. But we're not disappointed. As hot as it was and the way everyone's been running, that's about what we expected. Sure, you always want to run faster.

IF YOU RUN 212.1, YOU WANT TO RUN 212.2.

Maybe if it had been cooler, we could have picked up two-tenths of a second, and that is a big difference. But as I said, we're not disappointed."

—BILL ELLIOTT AFTER SETTING THE ALL-TIME NASCAR QUALIFYING RECORD[14]

dust. There was a big push to try to make the cars a little more aerodynamic, and we were also getting educated about how to build a more aerodynamic race car.

"Bill Elliott's car was the epitome of craftsmanship and what a football shape does for you. That little car would haul the mail. . . . It really would."

Of course, it was about more than aerodynamics. Elliott's cars typically were blessed with superb chassis setups. Horsepower was ample. And then there was Elliott himself: smoother than smooth.

But it was the smoothness of the T-Birds' lines that many considered the foundation.

Consider this: Elliott and his T-Birds set new standards for speed, especially at NASCAR's biggest tracks—Daytona International Speedway and Talladega Superspeedway. Elliott still holds the qualifying record at both of those tracks—210.364 miles per hour at Daytona, 212.809 at Talladega. Those records stand today because of the advent in 1988 of carburetor restrictor plates at those tracks. The plates, a significant safety initiative, reduce horsepower considerably.

Elliott drove the T-Bird to the "Winston Million" in 1985, a million-dollar bonus awarded by series sponsor R.J. Reynolds. To win the million, a driver needed to win three of the designated "big four" events: the Daytona 500, the World 600 at Charlotte, the Winston 500 at Talladega, and the Southern 500 at Darlington. Elliott won at Daytona and Talladega, then clinched the big payoff by winning at Darlington.

But perhaps the best illustration of Elliott's talent—and the Thunderbird's package—came in 1988, the first year of the speed-sapping restrictor plates. Elliott and everyone else went a lot slower on

TOP: The era of Bill Elliott's astounding qualifying speeds was cut short in 1988 with NASCAR's introduction of the carburetor restrictor plate.
BOTTOM: The plate was mandated after an incident involving Bobby Allison at Talladega in 1987. Although no one was injured, NASCAR felt it was time to slow the cars down at Daytona and Talladega. The plates have been in effect at those two tracks ever since.

the big tracks, but at season's end he had captured his first and only championship.

He did so with the days of history-making in his rear-view mirror.

"Those Thunderbirds," Elliott said, "were something different than what we were used to seeing. And they were something that helped mold the sport.

"I don't think anybody really understood how hard that was at the time we did it. I mean, it might have looked easy from the outside but I tell everybody this—I've been more impressed with me running 210 at Daytona in the era that I did it than about anything else I've done through my career. To me, not having the technology like today and being able to accomplish that goal—bias ply tires, no down-force, the whole bit—it's a whole different evolution. We came in, we were a bunch of nobodies. We worked hard and raised the bar on the sport."

WHAT'S IN A NAME? AS IT TURNED OUT, EVERYTHING

Winston had been around as the sponsor of NASCAR's premier series since 1971. The new sponsorship resulted in a new trophy, appropriately dubbed the "Winston Cup."

Nonetheless, the official name of the series remained NASCAR Grand National until 1986, when the NASCAR Winston Cup Series officially began.

First, some history:

NASCAR's premier series began life in 1949 under the name "Strictly Stock Division," reflecting the rules under which the cars competed. The eight-race 1949 season was run under this moniker. The cars had to be stock with no modifications whatsoever, except for the removal of headlights. A seat belt was required as well as a belt or leather strap to hold the driver's door shut.

With the coming 1950 season, NASCAR founder Bill France Sr. felt the series' name should stand for more than the rules interpretation. He chose the name "Grand National" after English steeplechase horse racing. France said that "Grand National indicates superior qualities." The term caught on and the division was known as such for the next thirty-six years.

R.J. Reynolds came on board in 1971 as the

ABOVE: The first Winston Million—a million-dollar bonus for winning specific races—was won by Bill Elliott at Darlington's Southern 500 in 1985. The bonus would be offered for several more years and won quite a few times by such drivers as Jeff Gordon and Dale Earnhardt.
OPPOSITE: NASCAR racing became a nationally recognized sport thanks, in part, to Winston's participation beginning in 1972.

GRAND NATIONAL CIRCUIT

(LATE MODEL STRICTLY STOCK AMERICAN CARS IN RACES OF 100 MILES OR MORE)

DETROIT FAIR GROUNDS

DETROIT, MICH.

250-MILE ANNIVERSARY CLASSIC—$12,500.00 PURSE

SUNDAY, AUG. 12, 1951

50 STARTERS—1950-51 MODELS ONLY—10 CARS QUALIFY EACH DAY OF TIME TRIALS
TIME TRIALS DAILY FROM SAT. AUG. 4th THROUGH WED. AUG. 8th

DARLINGTON RACEWAY

DARLINGTON, S.C.

500-MILE ANNUAL CLASSIC—$25,000.00 PURSE

LABOR DAY, SEPT. 3, 1951

75 STARTERS—1950-51 MODELS ONLY—5 CARS QUALIFY EACH DAY OF TIME TRIALS
TIME TRIALS FROM WED. AUG. 22nd THROUGH SAT. SEPT. 1st

Grand National Circuit Races at Langhorne, Phoenix and other important American speedways
Schedules sent to all members—Also available at National Headquarters

MORE THAN $150,000.00 PRIZE MONEY FOR LATE MODEL RACES IN 1951
PLUS
MORE THAN $25,000.00 *WEEKLY* **IN SPORTSMEN AND MODIFIED DIVISIONS**

SPEEDWAY DIVISION

CHAMPIONSHIP-TYPE CARS WITH STOCK AMERICAN MOTORS AND TRANSMISSIONS
FULL PARTICULARS AVAILABLE AT NATIONAL HEADQUARTERS

Bill France
President

Bill Tuthill
Secretary

NATIONAL ASSOCIATION for STOCK CAR AUTO RACING, INC.

800 MAIN STREET, DAYTONA BEACH, FLA.   TEL. 2-1815

Sanctioning Body of America's Most Important Stock Car Races and Speed Events

---

SANCTIONING BODY of AMERICA'S MOST IMPORTANT STOCK CAR RACES and SPEED EVENTS

LARGEST ORGANIZATION IN THE HISTORY OF AMERICAN AUTO RACING

Champions for 1950 in Three National Divisions

GRAND NATIONAL CIRCUIT

CHAMPIONSHIP MODIFIED DIVISION

SPECIAL MODIFIED—SPORTSMEN'S DIVISION

(STATE CHAMPIONS IN THE SPORTSMEN'S DIVISION)

PREPARATIONS NOW BEING MADE FOR SPEED TRIALS ON THE FAMOUS DAYTONA BEACH MEASURED MILE — FOREIGN AND AMERICAN STOCK CARS

★   ★   ★

ALL EVENTS UNDER SUPERVISION OF NATIONAL STOCK CAR RACING COMMISSION

★   ★   ★

E. G. "CANNONBALL" BAKER — *National Commissioner*

NATIONAL ASSOCIATION for STOCK CAR AUTO RACING, INC.

800 MAIN STREET, DAYTONA BEACH, FLORIDA

BILL TUTHILL, *National Secretary*

series' major sponsor using the name of its premier product—Winston cigarettes—to back selected events. In 1972 the sponsorship was expanded to include all races for the foreseeable future. In light of Winston's long-term commitment to the sport, the series' name was formally changed to the NASCAR Winston Cup Grand National Division beginning with the 1972 season. A subtle change to NASCAR Winston Cup Grand National Series was instituted in 1976.

The series' name was officially changed to the NASCAR Winston Cup Series as the 1986 season approached, and for the first time since 1950, the term Grand National was no longer associated with NASCAR's premier series.

NASCAR president Bill France made an announcement: "The NASCAR Winston Cup series has reached the pinnacle in motorsports. Fans throughout the world have come to recognize the "Winston Cup" name. We feel our friends at Winston deserve a name all their own. Winston's efforts have been the most significant in the progress of NASCAR and NASCAR-sanctioned tracks over the past fifteen years."

The name NASCAR Winston Cup Series was used through the 2003 season, with Nextel becoming the major sponsor in 2004.

DARRELL WALTRIP: A VOICE BEFORE HIS TIME

In retrospect, Darrell Waltrip could've let his driving do his talking for him.

But, if he had done that, just think about all the excitement we would've missed.

Waltrip is remembered first and foremost for his three championships (1981, 1982, 1985) in NASCAR's premier series, driving for Junior Johnson—an emergence that, following Cale Yarborough's three consecutive titles from 1976 to 1978, effectively ended the reign of "The King," Richard Petty.

Waltrip not only won but he reminded people he had won, and predicted more wins to come—he didn't come by the nickname "Jaws" accidentally. Sandpaper against the grain of old-line NASCAR, the youthful

OPPOSITE: Ads from 1950 and '51 show the premier NASCAR series being named the Grand National Circuit. The name was later changed to the NASCAR Winston Cup Series and today is known as the NASCAR Nextel Cup Series.
ABOVE: With Winston's sponsorship came signage and advertising for NASCAR events nationwide. This photo shows the old scoreboard at Talladega.

ABOVE: Darrell Waltrip celebrates in Daytona's Victory Lane after winning the biggest race of his career, the 1989 Daytona 500. He had tried to capture the Daytona crown sixteen times before. He won on his seventeenth try. His car number was 17.

OPPOSITE: Ford Motor Company introduced its super-sleek, re-engineered Thunderbird in 1983. It was a major effort on the factory's part to have a competitive car on the NASCAR circuit. More and more, aerodynamics were playing a role in the sport of stock car racing, and Ford was on the cutting edge with its advanced design.

Darrell Waltrip did not go down easily, especially because of the frequency of his victories. He ended up with eighty-four wins, tied with Bobby Allison for third-best all-time, behind only Richard Petty (200) and David Pearson (105). When he became the first driver to win one million dollars in a season in 1985, well, he talked that up, too.

Of course, time healed those wounds, both in the garage and in the grandstands.

Waltrip became the admired veteran when he finally won the Daytona 500 in 1988, after sixteen frustrating attempts, driving the "Tide Machine" Chevrolet. He then evolved into the elder statesman in the last few years of his racing career, which paved the way for a second—and current—career, that of television color commentator for NASCAR broadcasts.

Waltrip, with his now-trademark "boogity, boogity, boogity" first-lap call, has become one of the sport's most recognizable faces.

Again.

NASCAR SUPERCARS

1980s: Ford Thunderbird

- **TOP DRIVER:** Bill Elliott

- **OTHER MEMORABLE DRIVERS:**
  Cale Yarborough, Kyle Petty, Ricky Rudd,
  Buddy Baker, Mark Martin, Davey Allison

- **RACES WON:** 53

- **CHAMPIONSHIPS:**
  Elliott in 1988

NOTABLE: The supercar designation applies to an incarnation of the T-Bird introduced in 1983. The car had a radical, rounded, aerodynamic package that ushered in a new era for NASCAR—and production cars. Elliott and his T-Birds set all-time qualifying speed records that still stand at Daytona International Speedway (210.364 mph) and Talladega Superspeedway (212.809).

UNDER CONSTRUCTION: THE LEGEND OF DALE EARNHARDT

After a stunning introduction into NASCAR—winning the Rookie of the Year title in 1979, then winning the premier series championship in 1980—Dale Earnhardt faded in the first half of the decade.

Then, in 1984, he hooked up full-time with car owner Richard Childress, winning two races, more than $600,000, and finishing fourth in the series points—somewhat under-the-radar as far as the casual fan was concerned, but within NASCAR, the word was out: a championship combination had been formed.

The championships came, in 1986 and 1987, with Earnhardt coming to embody not one nickname but two—"Ironhead" and "The Intimidator"—with a derring-do style reminiscent of his short-track ace father, Ralph Earnhardt.

OPPOSITE: With Ford's design efforts focused on racing, General Motors followed suit with the introduction of its Chevrolet Monte Carlo "Aerocoupe" (shown here) and Pontiac's 2+2 in 1986. Pontiac had a new Grand Prix in 1988, and Chevy's design prevailed through '89 when the Chevrolet Lumina was introduced. Chevy went back to the newly remodeled Monte Carlo in 1995, and it has been the model of choice ever since. Ford dropped the T-Bird in 1998, and has been using the Taurus body style since that time.
RIGHT: "The Intimidator," Dale Earnhardt, is a classic American success story. He came from humble means to accomplish great wealth and worldwide recognition by doing his job better than anyone else.

As the decade evolved and the championships were won, the shy country boy acquired a swagger and aura that belied his humble beginnings and lack of formal education. Earnhardt eventually would be as comfortable in boardrooms as he was in prerace driver's meetings. The 1980s provided the competitive success that spurred such personal development and helped make him a true *personality*.

The leader on the track, Earnhardt also became the leader in the garage, an unofficial liaison between competitors and NASCAR officials. His was a voice always heard—and listened to.

As the decade came to a close, Earnhardt had three titles. And with Waltrip aging, the wondrous talent Tim Richmond passing away, and Bill Elliott fading slightly, Earnhardt had become the pre-eminent driver in NASCAR's premier series.

Despite that, there was a gaping hole in an ever expanding résumé. En route to winning championships, Earnhardt was also becoming more proficient than anyone, ever, at winning races held on Daytona International Speedway's 2.5-mile tri-oval. At the same time, he was developing a remarkable knack for being unable to win the Daytona 500.

TOP: The Intimidator's mentor and father, Ralph Earnhardt. He was among the fiercest competitors.
BOTTOM: NASCAR's rookie class of 1979. Bottom row, left to right: Geoff Bodine, Harry Gant, and Terry Labonte. Top row, left to right: Joe Milliken, Dale Earnhardt, Dave Watson, and Connie Saylor. Stiff competition, but Earnhardt beat them all for the rookie title.
OPPOSITE: 1987 NASCAR champion Dale Earnhardt flanked by his wife, Teresa. It was Earnhardt's third and last championship in the 1980s.

1987
Winston Cup Champion

"It was hard as hell [to keep losing the Daytona 500]. I mean, there was times he'd run out of the house screaming. There's times when you just did not know what to do with yourself. I mean, because I don't know, when we all wanted him to win it so bad . . . he lost it in the third turn [in 1990] with that flat tire and that was probably the hardest one because he just dominated that race and had a twenty-two-second lead at one point. To see him get spun off out off of Turn 2 a couple times, racing for second, you know, wasn't no fun either . . . I know,

IT WAS TOUGH ON ALL OF US. . . .

It was not a whole lot of fun back then. "

—DALE EARNHARDT JR. ON THE FRUSTRATION HIS FATHER
EXPERIENCED PRIOR TO FINALLY WINNING THE DAYTONA 500 IN 1998[15]

Such Daytona disparity—it was at once confusing and compelling. The greatest driver in NASCAR could not win NASCAR's greatest race. That disparity would be the dominant topic of discussion among fans for the remainder of Earnhardt's career.

INTERNATIONAL, PART I: NASCAR IN AUSTRALIA

NASCAR's first trip outside the continental United States came in 1987 when an exhibition race was held at the Calder Park Thunderdome in Sanbury, Australia. The race pitted some of NASCAR's stars against the local Aussie talent. Some of the drivers from down under, such as Allan Grice and Dick Johnson, raced stateside in NASCAR's premier series in order to prepare for the race. A crowd of 46,000 witnessed the NASCAR Goodyear International 500K on February 28, 1987.

Morgan Shepherd won the $250,000 event in a RahMoc-prepared Pontiac. He described the track as "a little like Bristol, a little like Dover, a little like Rockingham, and a little like Charlotte." Allan Grice had the best Australian showing, finishing eighth.

The second trip to Australia came on December 18, 1988—The NASCAR Goodyear 500K—again held at Calder. Michael Waltrip, Sterling Marlin, Herschel McGriff, Kyle Petty, and Bobby Allison were some

Morgan Shepherd, winner of the 1987 NASCAR Goodyear 500K in Australia.

of the NASCAR stars that competed. A sprinkling of West Coast and ARCA stars also appeared. One of the biggest names in the event was Neil Bonnett, in his first race following injuries from a Charlotte accident in October 1987. Bonnett took command of the race in another RahMoc Pontiac and won the final NASCAR-Australia set of races.

The Australian races were fun but logistically problematic. Australian trips were discontinued after the 1988 race. However, NASCAR had gone international and would journey abroad again in the late 1990s with a trio of races in Japan.

EVER EVOLVING: THE NASCAR BUSCH SERIES

The NASCAR Busch Series—the current label for the nation's second-most popular motorsports series began as the NASCAR Sportsman Division in 1950. The name was maintained until 1968 when the name NASCAR Late Model Sportsman Division was first used. Among some of the early champions were Ralph Earnhardt, Red Farmer, Ned Jarrett, and Morgan Shepherd.

Another name change came about in 1982 when the Anheuser-Busch company joined with NASCAR to create a schedule of approximately thirty races per year. The series was known as the Budweiser Late Model Sportsman Series and became the Busch Late Model Sportsman Series in 1984.

The next change came in 1986 when NASCAR dropped the term "Grand National" from its premier

division, which became known as NASCAR Winston Cup, and transferred the term to the Sportsman cars.

Some footnotes: The name "NASCAR Busch Grand National Series" was used through 1993. The series was known as the NASCAR Busch Series, Grand National Division from 1994 to '02. A final change took place in 2003 when the current name, NASCAR Busch Series, was adopted.

THE 1988 NASCAR BUSCH GRAND NATIONAL SERIES

The SERIES: The NASCAR Busch Grand National Series began its present format in 1982 when Anheuser-Busch, Inc., through its Budweiser brand, sponsored the Late Model Sportsman Series. In 1984, Busch Beer took the sponsorship over for the Series. In 1986, NASCAR placed the name Grand National, instead of Late Model Sportsman, to our Series. In six seasons, and only 178 events, the NASCAR Busch Grand National Series has become one of the fastest growing and most competitive racing series in the country. In 1987 alone, the NASCAR Busch Grand National Series produced fifteen (15) different race winners, the most in its six year history. Also, the Busch Series showed a 20% attendance growth over the 1986 season although there were five fewer races on the schedule. In 1988, the NASCAR Busch Grand National Series will consist of 30 races at 19 different tracks in 11 different states.

The TRACKS: The 1988 NASCAR Busch Grand National Series will be run on tracks that vary in length from the .333 mile Oxford Plains Speedway to the 2.5 mile Daytona International Speedway. In all, six super-speedways (tracks one mile or over in length) and thirteen (13) short tracks (tracks less than one mile in length) will host Busch Series events.

The CARS: Eligible cars for the 1988 BGN Series fall into three groups:

GROUP I: 1986 Model cars with 105 inch wheelbase and max/min. treadwidth of 60 inches.
1986 Buick Century; Chevrolet Celebrity; Ford Thunderbird; Mercury Cougar; Olds Cutlass Ciera (Notch Back); & Pontiac 6000

GROUP II: 1986 Model cars with either 105 or 112 inch wheelbase and max/min. treadwidth of 60 inches.
Buick (LeSabre, Regal Coupe); Chevrolet (Monte Carlo, Monte Carlo SS, Monte Carlo Aerocoupe); Olds (Cutlass 442, Delta 88); Pontiac (Grand Prix, Grand Prix 2+2).

NOTE: Only cars with 105 inch wheelbase will be permitted to compete on tracks of less than 1 mile in length.

GROUP III: Limited to 1975 through 1980 intermediate size cars that must maintain a 112 inch wheelbase and may compete on tracks of 1 mile or over in length.
Buick - '75-'79 Apollo; Chevrolet - '75-'79 Nova/'78-'80 Malibu; Ford - '78-'80 Fairmont; Olds - '75-'79 Omega; Pontiac - '75-'80 Ventura/'78-'80 Grand Prix, LeMans, and Grand Am

The MONEY: In 1988, the NASCAR Busch Grand National Series will be worth a total of approximately $3 million in race purses and sponsor point fund money. The 1988 Champion will receive approximately $80,000 in additional point fund and sponsor contingency money. Anheuser-Busch, Inc. will post a $100,000 point fund in 1988 to be shared by the top twenty drivers at seasons end. Also, Busch Beer will again sponsor a pole award at each of the 30 races worth $300 to the fastest qualifier.

OPPOSITE TOP: Neil Bonnett wheeled this RahMoc-prepared Pontiac to victory in the 1988 NASCAR Australian race.
OPPOSITE BOTTOM: Dale Earnhardt and car builder Robert Gee celebrate a victory in the first NASCAR Busch Series race (Daytona, 1982). Gee was known as the "Michelangelo" of car builders. He also was the maternal grandfather of Dale Earnhardt Jr.
RIGHT: NASCAR introduced the NASCAR Busch Series in 1982. This is an overview of the series from 1988.

CHAPTER SIX

1990s

CHANGE BECOMES THE BYWORD

Change was the byword as NASCAR entered the 1990s. Change was everywhere for a sport growing up so fast, in so many directions, all at once. Vision—meaning the vision of founder Bill France Sr.—had mutated throughout the years.

NASCAR was ever-moving toward nationwide acceptance as a mainstream sport.

But with such movement came the inevitable question, one that had been asked for decades beforehand, one destined to be asked forever, really. The question was posed, as always, by the non-believers or, at best, by those who simply could not grasp the allure of racing, much less the all-out *need* for speed.

Is auto racing a sport?

NASCAR had answers.

The answers came in the form of full fields and packed grandstands, the latter evidencing an increasing fan base that reflected diversity in gender, race, and socioeconomic status.

One answer was a simple "yes," that NASCAR racing was indeed a sport, based on its basic competitive aspects and the competitive instincts of its drivers, who were athletes, by God, albeit nontraditional ones.

To the more ardent naysayers there was another potential answer to offer up. This answer required acknowledging that, maybe, just maybe, NASCAR wasn't a sport.

But . . . maybe it was much more important than that.

Hurtling full-bore toward its destiny, NASCAR had support for the bigger-than-sport argument. Corporate involvement, exceeding that in any other major sport, had given races ramifications that reached off the race track. The inherent danger of driving a race car surrounded by forty or so other race cars for several hours at a time also raised the stakes beyond mere sport, didn't it?

This logic was the reverse of Hemingway's postulate that placed only three activities—bullfighting, mountain climbing, and auto racing—in the category of "sports." All the rest, Hemingway surmised, are games.

Either way, you get the point. NASCAR was elevating itself into the rarified air of the national consciousness. Be it a sport, be it a game, be it something beyond both—it was inconsequential.

PAGE 154: Jeff Gordon wins the 1997 Daytona 500.
TOP: Richard Petty "spread the NASCAR gospel" for nearly five decades and according to a 1992 issue of *Stock Car Racing* magazine, was one of the ten most trusted people in the world.
OPPOSITE: NASCAR's only seven-time champions compete against each other during the 1992 Pyroil 500K at Phoenix. Petty was one race away from his retirement.

A RACE FOR THE AGES . . .

Someone could've written a book about the season-ending race of 1992.

Come to think of it, someone did.

Actually, a book by *Charlotte Observer* motorsports writer David Poole addressed the 1992 season overall, but of course paid particular attention to the November 12 finale at Atlanta Motor Speedway, to a Sunday afternoon drenched in dynamics.

"It would be ten years before we got the full impact of that race," Poole wrote. "So many unbelievable things came together that day. It was just an incredible confluence of events."

The drama of that afternoon, on the surface, was statistically driven. Below the surface, there were implications galore, though several would play out retroactively during a 1993 season tinged with tragedy.

As far as the stats went, coming into the event, six drivers were in mathematical contention for the series championship. In descending order, they were: Davey Allison, Alan Kulwicki, Bill Elliott, Harry Gant, Kyle Petty, and Mark Martin. Realistically, though, it was an Allison-Kulwicki-Elliott showdown, as those three were separated by merely thirty points.

Allison wrecked early, taking him out of the hunt and leaving things to Kulwicki and Elliott. Kulwicki, a degreed-engineer-turned-driver from Wisconsin, driving an underfunded No. 7 Thunderbird—they called

Race cars gleam with colors reflecting their Fortune 500 company sponsorships. As the sport grew to capture national attention, major companies realized the great "bang for the buck" value of NASCAR racing.

" Alan was better than me for the thirty to thirty-five laps on new tires. Then I would be better than him for the next thirty to thirty-five laps. I felt if I could keep him within a couple of seconds when he was on new tires, I could beat him at the end if the race went green. That's the way it ended up, but he knew exactly what he had to do. He came in here with ten points over me and

I NEEDED SOMEONE TO BE BETWEEN HIM AND ME AT THE END.

But that just didn't happen. **"**

—BILL ELLIOTT ON WINNING THE 1992 HOOTERS 500
BUT LOSING THE NASCAR CHAMPIONSHIP TO ALAN KULWICKI[16]

it the "Underbird" because of that—became a master tactician down the stretch of the race.

A season-long points battle came down to the five-point bonus for leading the most laps in an event. Kulwicki and his team monitored that "race within the race" and when the No. 7 had led 103 laps with 18 laps remaining, they knew they had the title clinched.

Kulwicki pitted while leading; Elliott took the lead and motored on to victory, with Kulwicki finishing second. Elliott ended up leading 102 laps of the 328-lap race. Thus, Kulwicki won the championship by only ten points.

"There's never been a race more remarkable, in the way things played out," wrote Poole.

Get this: If Elliott had led the most laps that day, *he* would've gotten the five-point bonus, leaving he and Kulwicki tied in points overall. The first tiebreak is victories in a season; Elliott would've taken the title because he won more races in 1992 than Kulwicki.

The closest points battle in the history of NASCAR's premier series had several subplots that

LEFT: All great things must come to an end, and the most successful driving career in racing history came to an end on November 15, 1992. Richard Petty hung up his helmet after Atlanta's Hooters 500. It was a career that spanned thirty-four years, seven championships, and two hundred wins. On this day, as one career was laid to rest, another was being born. Jeff Gordon's first start in NASCAR's premier series was in this very race.
OPPOSITE TOP: Richard and Lynda Petty take a ceremonial victory lap before the 1992 Pyroil 500K at Phoenix, Arizona. Petty would finish twenty-fourth this day and retire two weeks later.
OPPOSITE BOTTOM: Alan Kulwicki on his way to the 1992 NASCAR Winston Cup championship. Kulwicki, driving his Hooters "Underbird," was the first independent owner-driver to win the championship since Rex White did it in 1960.

have become both more interesting and saddening with the passage of time.

The 1992 Hooters 500 was the final race in Richard Petty's long and glorious career. He wrecked early in the event, his car briefly catching fire. "I wanted to go out in a blaze of glory, but not like that," Petty said. The No. 43 Pontiac was brought to the garage and worked on for more than two hours, enabling Petty to return for the final lap, giving fans a proper, final goodbye.

You want implications? Petty's last race was also Jeff Gordon's first as far as racing in NASCAR's premier series was concerned. Gordon, fresh off a record-setting eleven-pole rookie year in the NASCAR Busch Series, drove the finale for car owner Rick Hendrick. He started twenty-first and finished thirty-first, a nondescript run on an otherwise extraordinary day.

Kulwicki quickly became an immensely popular champion: with the image of an intelligent, introspective NASCAR outsider, he was embraced by fans. His popularity made his death the following spring, when his plane crashed en route to Bristol Motor Speedway, all the more saddening.

Kulwicki was flying to Bristol from an autograph session in Knoxville, Tennessee, one of those events that had underscored his growing populist appeal. Shortly before the turbo-prop craft was scheduled to land at the small Tri-Cities Airport, there was a mechanical malfunction and the plane plummeted to the ground, killing Kulwicki, Hooters executive Mark Brooks, sports marketing director Dan Duncan, and pilot Charlie Campbell.

Davey Allison, who many had considered the favorite going into the 1992 finale, likewise left this

world in 1993. And like Kulwicki, he had become one of NASCAR's most beloved figures, a status elevated considerably by the empathy felt for his family. His brother Clifford had died in August 1992 during a NASCAR Busch Series practice session at Michigan International Speedway. Allison patriarch Bobby Allison nearly died in a 1988 accident at Pocono Raceway, a wreck that ended his career. Bobby had since returned to the race track, unable to compete but undeniably committed to watching his sons do so.

Davey Allison was certain to do his father's legacy—and his brother's memory—proud. A championship, driving for Robert Yates, surely would come soon, to be followed by who knew how many?

Three months after Kulwicki's death, Davey Allison was involved in a severe helicopter crash—he was the pilot—in the infield of Talladega Superspeedway. He died the next day.

At that point, the book had been closed on the implications of the 1992 season finale.

Or so it was thought.

"You look back at the race and the Richard Petty story looks like a subtext," Poole wrote. "But at the time, it was the story coming out of that day."

Time proved that the day's other stories were at least as important.

LEFT: Second-generation driver Davey Allison shows off hardware won in the 1992 Pyroil 500K at Phoenix. Allison was the 1987 Rookie of the Year, scoring his first win during his rookie season. He had nineteen wins before his death in a 1993 helicopter accident.
OPPOSITE: Alan Kulwicki, the guy who did it his way. Although offered several very good rides with top teams, Kulwicki chose to run his own operation.

The 1992 season finale, Poole added, was a fitting punctuation to a year that was eventful from the outset and stands as a watershed year for NASCAR.

"Bill France Sr. died; NASCAR tested at Indianapolis for the first time; the radial tire came in; and then you had Atlanta," wrote Poole. "So many things happened that year."

MOVE OVER, EARNHARDT: BOY WONDER USHERS IN NEW ORDER

Jeff Gordon had forsaken his roots and in the process forsaken everything once held as holy in American auto racing. USAC to NASCAR? The ultimate detour, wasn't it, this switch to the Southeast, away from the Midwest and mecca, otherwise known to racers as Indianapolis Motor Speedway?

But Jeff Gordon was a living, breathing, 180-mile-per-hour detour—born in California but raised in Indiana, a Tom Cruise lookalike who drove like the Cruise character Cole Trickle in the movie *Days of Thunder.*

Jeff Gordon arrived at the perfect time. And he arrived with a perfect car owner—Rick Hendrick—who had sensed the success that lay ahead and had hired Gordon away from the clutches of other operations. Gordon also arrived with the perfect crew chief, Ray Evernham, who was bent on causing as much noise off the track as Gordon was on it. Evernham was responsible for creation of the "Rainbow Warriors," a new-and-improved version of the NASCAR pit crew, featuring workers dedicated to over-the-wall speed and precision. Their nickname came from the bright

multicolored uniforms and car paint scheme, via title sponsor DuPont.

They complemented their driver perfectly, as Gordon won Rookie of the Year honors in 1993, then captured series championships in '95, '97, and '98 (he added a fourth championship in 2001). In '98 he tied Richard Petty's modern-era record for victories in a season, with thirteen.

Along the way, he even married a "Miss Winston," Brooke Sealey.

Storybook stuff it was, coinciding with NASCAR's continued growth and the inevitable slide of seven-time champion Dale Earnhardt. It was a development that divided much of NASCAR's fervent fan base.

Much like Darrell Waltrip had ten years before,

Rick Hendrick–owned cars finished first, second, and fourth in the 1989 Daytona 500, but Hendrick scored a trifecta in 1997 when his cars finished one-two-three. Jeff Gordon (center) won the 500, with Terry Labonte (left) second, and Ricky Craven (right) coming home third.

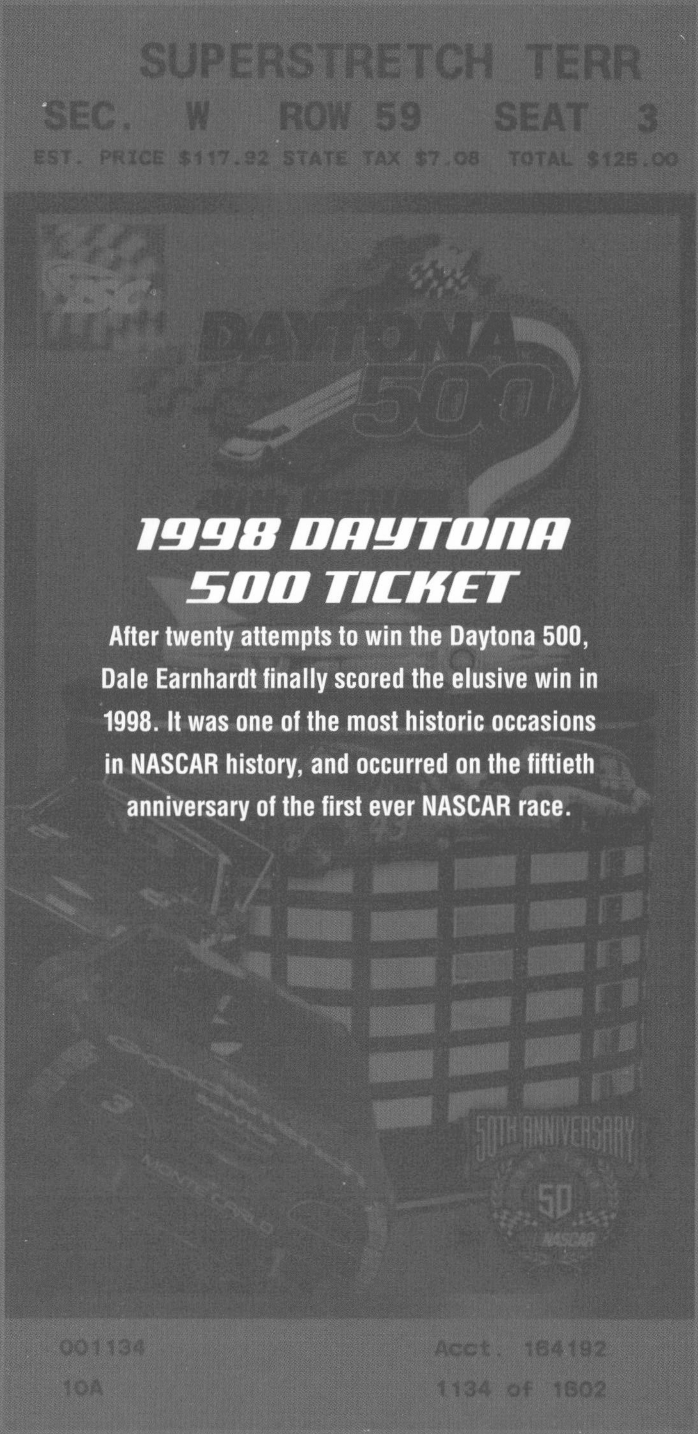

SUPERSTRETCH TERR
SEC. W ROW 59 SEAT 3
EST. PRICE $117.92 STATE TAX $7.08 TOTAL $125.00
DAYTONA 500
50TH ANNIVERSARY
001134
Acct. 164192
10A
1134 of 1602

1998 DAYTONA 500 TICKET

After twenty attempts to win the Daytona 500, Dale Earnhardt finally scored the elusive win in 1998. It was one of the most historic occasions in NASCAR history, and occurred on the fiftieth anniversary of the first ever NASCAR race.

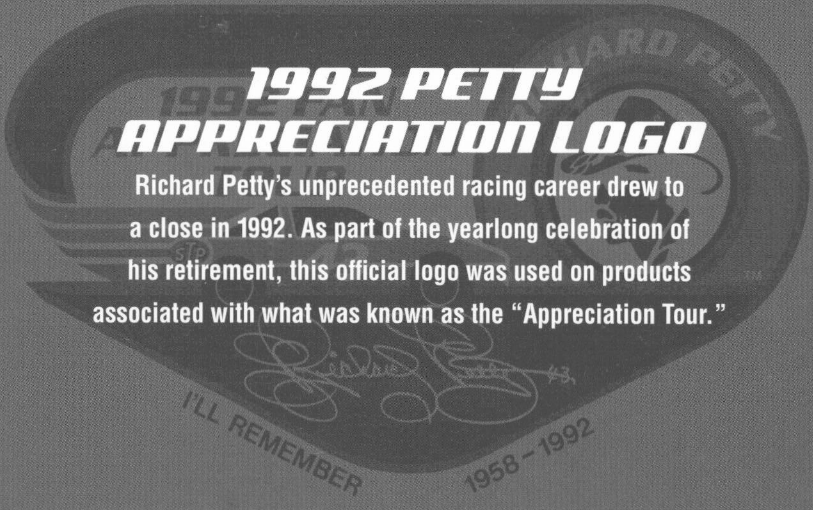

RICHARD PETTY
I'LL REMEMBER
1958-1992

1992 PETTY APPRECIATION LOGO

Richard Petty's unprecedented racing career drew to a close in 1992. As part of the yearlong celebration of his retirement, this official logo was used on products associated with what was known as the "Appreciation Tour."

1999 NASCAR WINSTON CUP SERIES ANNUAL PRESS CONFERENCE INVITATION
NASCAR

INVITATION TO 1999 MEDIA EVENT

This creative invitation was sent to members of the media for a 1999 Winston press conference.

" I want to be like

RICHARD PETTY AND DALE EARNHARDT,

and make a name for myself in this series. To come here in a stock car and win, it's the greatest thing that's ever happened to me. **"**

—A THEN TWENTY-THREE-YEAR-OLD JEFF GORDON, AFTER WINNING THE INAUGURAL BRICKYARD 400 AT INDIANAPOLIS MOTOR SPEEDWAY IN 1994[17]

Gordon became the driver many fans loved to hate, because of a bold brashness that aggravated many a ticket-buyer. Gordon took it in cool, Cruise-like stride, and even learned to love the boos directed his way during prerace introductions.

"If they ever stop booing me," Gordon said, "that'll tell me something. It'll be a sign that I must not be doing so well, because they won't be mad at me anymore."

1994 BRICKYARD 400: A SUPERSTAR UNVEILED

Three series championships amounted to premature Hall of Fame status for Gordon. Victories in the Brickyard 400 in 1994 and '98 amounted to symmetry (he won again in 2001). Gordon, back home in Indiana, was an Indianapolis champion after all, just not in the type of cars originally envisioned.

The first Brickyard 400 victory for Gordon was most memorable because, well, it was the first Brickyard 400—a long-awaited NASCAR debut at the world's most famous race track.

The Indianapolis Motor Speedway was hallowed ground as far as the die-hard open-wheel racing fan was concerned. After all, the track had been in existence since 1909. Nothing but exotic Indy Cars had touched its fabled surface, both brick and asphalt, since those first days.

The thought of a race at this shrine featuring stock cars was unthinkable.

Ray Evernham and his crew, the "Rainbow Warriors," celebrate Jeff Gordon's Daytona 500 win in 1997. Motor Racing Network's announcer Jim Phillips looks for an interview.

But Big Bill France thought about it for most of his life.

France had cut his racing teeth in the early 1930s driving ancient, open-wheeled sprint cars on the primitive dirt tracks of rural Maryland. He worked on several pit crews at Indy during the 1930s, and was a member of George Robson's 1946 Indianapolis 500 winning team, just one year before France founded NASCAR. He dreamed of the day when his NASCAR boys would race at the world's greatest race course.

That day came on August 6, 1994, the day of the first Brickyard 400. Unfortunately, it was two years after Big Bill's death, but his long-held dream had come true and the present-day NASCAR drivers would be the beneficiaries.

Among those drivers was Gordon, who like Big Bill had dreamed of racing at Indy. Stock cars or Indy cars, it didn't matter to Gordon. He was here to make the "big show." And make the show he did, qualifying in third spot.

Race day dawned bright, hot, and sunny. The race was a sellout, much to the chagrin of the open-wheel purists. A field of forty-three stock cars rumbled down the front-stretch canyon of grandstands as the green flag flew. Gordon took the lead on Lap 3, and held it

OPPOSITE: Jeff Gordon wins the 1995 Pepsi 400 at Daytona. Gordon's roots are in Midwest sprint car and midget racing. He was among the first of a number of open-wheel drivers who looked to NASCAR for a big-league racing career. Ryan Newman, Casey Mears, Tony Stewart, and Robby Gordon are among the former open-wheel stars who followed Jeff Gordon's lead into NASCAR.

RIGHT: Jeff Gordon rocked the racing world almost from his first start. He was the "real deal," as they say. He's shown here in 1994.

to lap twenty-four for his first of seven stints at the front of the pack. Thirteen drivers swapped the lead a total of twenty-one times during the 160-lap event, which was slowed six times for twenty-five laps, due to accidents, none of which were serious.

As the checkered flag fell, it was Jeff Gordon making history and establishing himself as a superstar, winning the first stock car race ever held on the eighty-five-year-old speedway. Gordon took home $613,000 for the victory after outdueling Ernie Irvan down the stretch, then—after Irvan had to pit with a flat tire—nipping runner-up Brett Bodine by 0.53 seconds.

TIME FOR TRUCKIN': NASCAR CRAFTSMAN TRUCK SERIES HITS THE TRACK

In 1995 the NASCAR Craftsman Truck Series was born, becoming NASCAR's third national series. Immediately, it was a huge hit with fans throughout the country because of its door-to-door competition between drivers who, for the most part, aspired to advance through the competitive ranks to either the NASCAR Busch Series or NASCAR's premier series (now known as NASCAR Nextel Cup).

Originally, the notion of a truck series seemed aimed toward a "companion" series role, supporting the NASCAR Winston West Series. Car owner Jimmy Smith was one of the leaders in building momentum for the concept.

In February 1994 Smith took a racing pick-up prototype to Daytona Beach, Florida, during the annual Speed Weeks extravaganza held at Daytona

International Speedway. Smith's truck attracted a huge amount of attention and helped precipitate a meeting with NASCAR officials to discuss the possibility of a viable truck-race series.

Soon, the truck series virtually took on a life of its own. And when it got the "green light" from NASCAR, things moved lightning-fast. In the spring of 1994, NASCAR announced the formation of the "NASCAR SuperTruck Series presented by Craftsman."

The involvement of a big-time sponsor was complemented by the involvement of some big-name teams—Richard Childress Racing, Dale Earnhardt, Inc., and Rick Hendrick Motorsports. Also jumping in and fielding teams were drivers Geoffrey Bodine and Ernie Irvan.

Several demonstration races were held during the second half of 1994, followed by some winter exhibitions. All told, race fans were able to witness a total of seven previews to what would become an exciting addition to NASCAR's competitive scene.

The series' first race was held at Phoenix International Raceway on February 5, 1995. Mike Skinner won that event, which got him started toward winning the series' first championship.

In 1996 Craftsman's involvement changed from a presenting sponsor to a title sponsor, creating a new series name: the NASCAR Craftsman Truck Series.

From its inception, the series has been an intriguing mix of youthful drivers and veterans. The series' list of champions, starting with Skinner, holds some of NASCAR's biggest names—Ron Hornaday Jr. (champion in 1996 and '98), Jack Sprague ('97, '99, '01), Greg Biffle ('00), and Mike Bliss ('02).

It also currently features a rising star, 2003 titlist Travis Kvapil.

THE INTIMIDATOR FINALLY TAKES THE BIG ONE

Dale Earnhardt hit the ground running when he came to NASCAR's premier series. He won the Rookie of the Year Award in 1979, his first full season. He went on to win his first of seven series championships the following year. No other driver has ever accomplished

OPPOSITE TOP: Ron Hornaday Jr. leads the field through Turn I at Homestead-Miami Speedway.
OPPOSITE BOTTOM: Mike Skinner celebrates his win in the first NASCAR Truck Series event ever held (Phoenix, 1995).
ABOVE: The series was known as the NASCAR Super Truck Series back then. Jack Sprague was the series champ in 1997, '99 and '01.

ABOVE: In an unprecedented show of congratulations, crew members and officials line up to shake the hand of Dale Earnhardt, as he makes his way to Victory Lane after finally winning the Daytona 500 in his twentieth attempt.
OPPOSITE: "Wonder Boy," Jeff Gordon, gets quick service from his crew, the Rainbow Warriors, on his way to a win in Daytona Speedway's first night race, the 1998 Pepsi 400.
PAGE 174: Dale Earnhardt spins his tires on the infield of Daytona International Speedway in celebration of his first victory at the elusive Daytona 500.

those successes in consecutive years.

Earnhardt almost immediately began winning races on the superspeedways of the NASCAR world. His favorite track seemed to be the mammoth Daytona International Speedway, where he could run flat out—just the way he liked it. He would go on to hold the record for most wins at the legendary track—thirty-four—but for all his success, the premier event at the speedway, indeed the premier event in all of NASCAR, eluded him.

The Daytona 500.

Dale Earnhardt's first Daytona 500 was in 1979. He started tenth in Rod Osterlund's Buick and took the lead for the first time on Lap 44. He led four more times for a total of ten laps, finishing eighth, one lap down to race winner Richard Petty. Not bad for a maiden voyage.

Over the years "The Intimidator," as Earnhardt had become known, came close to winning his dream race. He was runner-up five times and looked like a sure winner in 1990 when he led going into Turn 3 on the last lap, only to have a rear tire blow due to debris on the track. Underdog Derrike Cope came home the winner as Earnhardt limped home in fifth place. Fans were beginning to wonder if The Intimidator was jinxed. After all, there were many great and famous drivers who should have won the Daytona 500 but always seemed to come up short.

NASCAR SUPERCARS

1980s and 1990s: Chevrolet Monte Carlo

•**TOP DRIVERS:** Dale Earnhardt and Jeff Gordon

•**OTHER MEMORABLE DRIVERS:**
Darrell Waltrip, Terry Labonte, Benny Parsons, Sterling Marlin, Tim Richmond

•**RACES WON:** 197

•**CHAMPIONSHIPS:**
A total of eight in the 1980s and 1990s–Earnhardt in 1980, 1986, and 1987; Waltrip in 1985; Labonte in 1996; Gordon in 1995, 1997, 1998.

NOTABLE: Monte Carlos have won more races than any other make in NASCAR's premier series (251 from 1980 through the end of the 2003 season) and interestingly, the make's dominance was halted from 1989 to 1994 by another Chevy model—the Lumina, which Earnhardt drove to four series championships.

" It was just like John Elway when he won the Super Bowl.

HE HAD THAT LOOK IN HIS EYES.

We [the Richard Childress team] came to Daytona with that same look in our eyes and we won. We proved we could win the Daytona 500. **"**

—DALE EARNHARDT ON WINNING THE 1998 DAYTONA 500[18]

DAYTONA 500

40th ANNUAL
FEBRUARY 15, 1998

Earnhardt and his Richard Childress Racing team came to Daytona with a new attitude in 1998. The 1997 race had been dismal: Earnhardt flipped on the backstretch of Lap 190 after tangling with Dale Jarrett. As Earnhardt was led to the ambulance for a check-up, he asked if his wrecked Chevy would fire up. A member of the track crew reached in the car and hit the switch. Sure enough, the black Monte Carlo barked to life. Earnhardt jumped in the battered mount and drove it back to the pits. After some repairs, he came back out on the track and finished the race in thirty-first.

That misfortune set an unfamiliar tone for Earnhardt. That season, for the first time in fifteen seasons, he went winless. In 1998 the team not only hoped the Daytona 500 would finally come its way, but viewed it as a potential springboard to an unprecedented eighth championship.

The morning of February 15, 1998, was dreary, with gray skies rolling in off the nearby Atlantic, blanketing the speedway but in no way dampening the enthusiasm of the 200,000-plus fans who came out to cheer their favorite drivers.

That day, incidentally, was also the fiftieth anniversary of NASCAR's first race.

Many in the stands hoped they would witness another kind of history, one involving Dale Earnhardt.

The familiar black GM Goodwrench No. 3 started fourth, outside in the second row. Earnhardt took the lead on Lap 17 and stayed near the front of the pack for most

LEFT: Program from the 1998 Daytona 500. The race was run on the 50th anniversary of NASCAR's first event.
OPPOSITE: Dale Earnhardt leads the pack, once a familiar sight on the NASCAR circuit.

light suddenly flashed as the pack roared down the backstretch for the final time—John Andretti and Lake Speed had tangled coming off Turn 2.

Earnhardt was only one turn away from fulfilling his lifelong dream of winning the world's greatest stock car race. There's no doubt the 1990 race flashed in his mind. This time it would be different. What had been, arguably, the most anticipated event in NASCAR history was only one mile away. NASCAR's elder statesman—in truth, a mellower version of The Intimidator—finally was about to cross the doorstep of Daytona 500 destiny.

Pandemonium broke out as Dale Earnhardt passed under the most important checkered flag of his career. As he came down pit road after the cool-down lap, nearly every person in the pit area came out to congratulate Earnhardt on a job well done. He spun a few donuts in the tri-oval grass and made his way to Victory Lane, a route with which he was very familiar.

He climbed atop his weary Chevy and acknowledged the praise from the cheering throng.

Suffice it to say that virtually *everyone* was a Dale Earnhardt fan that day.

INTERNATIONAL, PART II: NASCAR IN JAPAN

The inevitable international aspirations that were first realized with the 1988 race in Melbourne, Australia, truly came to fruition for NASCAR when the sanctioning body—represented by drivers primarily from its premier series, then called NASCAR Winston Cup—visited Japan for a series of three exhibition races during the late 1990s.

The first two events were held at the Suzuka

ABOVE: The official logo of NASCAR's 50th anniversary.
OPPOSITE: Dale Earnhardt celebrates the biggest win of his career, the 1998 Daytona 500.

of the race, leading four more times for a total of 107 laps, the most of any driver that day. It was looking good for Earnhardt. Of course, there had been many other years when it had looked good.

The crowd held its collective breath as the lead cars roared across the finish line to complete Lap 199, Earnhardt in front, with Bobby Labonte and Jeremy Mayfield nipping at his heels. The caution

"Today is an important milestone not only for NASCAR but also the U.S. automobile manufacturers. **FOR THE FIRST TIME IN OUR HISTORY,** we not only will be taking NASCAR-style racing to the heart of the Pacific Rim but we will be taking some of NASCAR's top drivers along to present our sport to a worldwide audience. NASCAR demonstration races in Japan will provide a tremendous platform for American automobile manufacturers and corporate sponsors to showcase their products in Japan."

—BILL FRANCE ON NASCAR RACING IN JAPAN[19]

road-race facility, the first taking place on November 24, 1996. It was billed as the NASCAR Suzuka Thunder Special 100.

In a shootout of legendary former series champions and longtime rivals, Rusty Wallace won the race by a margin of 1.192 seconds over runner-up Dale Earnhardt. A crowd of more than 40,000 saw Wallace totally dominate the one hundred-lap event.

Wallace started from the pole and led eighty-four of the one hundred laps. Wallace pocketed $130,940 for his efforts.

The second race in 1997, called the NASCAR Thunder Special—Suzuka, had a few "NASCAR firsts" connected to it. The drivers practiced and qualified in the rain, using Goodyear's new rain tire developed especially for the 3,400-pound stock cars, with the cars sporting windshield wipers and a red rear running light.

NASCAR used a European-style qualifying format with six groups of drivers, five cars in each group, taking to the track for three green-flag laps. Each driver's fastest lap was used to determine his starting position. Mark Martin took the pole for the 125-lap event over the 1.4-mile course.

Martin led 50 of the 125 laps, but it was 1996 Rookie of the Year Mike Skinner who won the race in his Richard Childress—owned Chevrolet.

Skinner described the track thusly:"It was real flat and not very fast. The only spot where you could go flat out was on the front straight into Turn 1. That part reminded me of Watkins Glen."

Program from the 1996 NASCAR race at Suzuka, Japan, the first of three NASCAR exhibition races held in Japan.

Skinner was extremely proud of the win, having beaten top road racers such as Martin and Rusty Wallace. But Skinner has fond memories of the event aside from winning.

"Christian Levendahl was my spotter that day," Skinner recalled. "He was a nephew of Mark Martin's. Christian really talked me around the track that day, in a sense, going head to head with his uncle. *We* won that one.

"The next year, Christian was killed in a car crash coming back from Richmond. He was a great guy and a good friend. That win will always be special for me."

The third and—to date—final NASCAR event in Japan was held at the new four hundred million–dollar Motegi Twin Ring racing complex in 1998. The track, located sixty miles outside Tokyo, features a 1.5-mile superspeedway oval and a road course. The race was called the NASCAR Thunder Special Motegi Coca-Cola 500.

Jeremy Mayfield won the pole with a speed of 158.799 miles per hour. Mayfield said the track was a mix of Pocono, Darlington, and Las Vegas. This race was historic in that it featured the first on-track meeting of Dale Earnhardt Sr. and Dale Earnhardt Jr. Junior finished sixth, beating out his dad, who came home eighth.

Once again Mike Skinner won, edging Jeff Gordon by 0.0153 seconds. Mayfield finished third, and Jeff Burton, in his Bruce Lee–sponsored Ford, came home fourth. According to Skinner, they won the race by using the right gear ratio.

"Curt and the guys really did their homework on the gear," Skinner said. "We had the option to shift or not to shift. They set it up for either way. An in-car

TOP: Rusty Wallace, winner of the first of three NASCAR exhibition races held in Japan.
BOTTOM: Mike Skinner won two of the three Japan races. He scored wins on Suzuka's road course and the Motegi superspeedway.
OPPOSITE: Action down the front stretch of the Suzuka, Japan, race course in 1996.

Winston 500

Sunday, May 2, 1993

Poulan Pro 500
IROC XVII
Sat., May 1, 1

DAVEY ALLISON
1992 Winston 500 Winner

1993 WINSTON 500 · TALLADEGA, AL

TALLADEGA SUPERSPEEDWAY

DAVEY ALLISON
1992 IROC XVI Winner

LEFT: Program from the 1993 Winston 500 at Talladega. Ironically, it was the last appearance by Davey Allison at his home track and he was featured on the cover.
BELOW: Press kit for the NASCAR Japan races.

ABOVE: Program from the 1993 Daytona 500.
RIGHT: Program from the 1996 Daytona 500. Dale Jarrett won both of these events. Jarrett also went on to win the 2000 Daytona 500.

camera was put in the car for the final practice, and everyone saw me shift.

"We tried to keep it quiet, but the next morning, there were transmissions strewn all the way down pit road. Everyone was changing trannies."

The only drawback to the Japan trips, according to Skinner, was the food. Japanese cuisine was not to his liking.

"If I lived there I'd be under 150 pounds," Skinner said. "On the way home I stopped in Hawaii for some golf and some American food."

Skinner had nothing but praise, however, for the Motegi circuit.

"Everything was first class," he said. "It is one of the nicest places I've been to. I can think of only one or two facilities here in the States which could even hold a candle to the Motegi track.

"The track has a strange shape, it kind of reminded me of Darlington Raceway a little. And the Japanese fans are the best. They were so gracious and polite. They love NASCAR racing."

The landmark trips to Japan not only put a bow tie on the 1990s for NASCAR, but also seemed to be in line with a Big Bill France prediction, which had come years before.

France's prophecy: "NASCAR will be as big as the stick-and-ball sports by the turn of the twenty-first Century."

At the threshold of the millennium, those words rang truer than ever.

OPPOSITE: Action during the 1996 NASCAR race at Suzuka, Japan.
RIGHT: Mike Helton, the first NASCAR president of the twenty-first century.

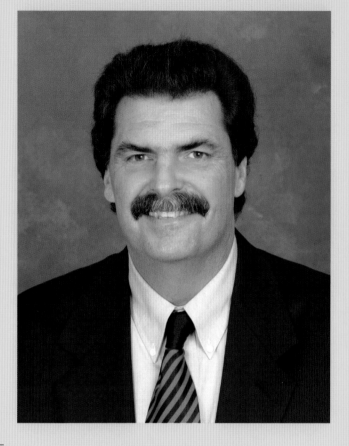

MR. PRESIDENT: HELTON AT THE HELM IN NEW CENTURY

Prior to November 2000, two men—one family— had held the presidential reins of NASCAR's high-speed operation. Bill France Sr. founded NASCAR in 1948 and led the company until 1972 when his son, also named Bill, took over. It was leadership lineage: father-to-son, blood-to-blood which went, of course, hand-in-hand.

All of which, in retrospect, made Mike Helton's emergence even more historic.

Helton took over as NASCAR president in the fall of 2000. Bill France relinquished that post and announced creation of a NASCAR Board of Directors, which he would chair.

Helton's move into the president's role followed a brief rise through the NASCAR ranks. From 1994-1999 he was the sanctioning body's vice president of competition; from 1999 until becoming president he was senior vice president and chief operating office. That latter job was also historic, as he then became the first person outside the France family to take over the day-to-day operation of NASCAR.

"When I go somewhere to speak, and I introduce myself as the President of NASCAR, it's a neat feeling," Helton said. "I like being able to say that."

Bill France liked saying this, on the day the transfer of power was announced: "Mike is well-suited to carry on the tradition of strong leadership at NASCAR, not only within our offices but for the entire industry."

EPILOGUE: NASCAR ALL ABOUT NEWNESS IN THE TWENTY-FIRST CENTURY

A new century, a new NASCAR—it amounts to a nice fit. Like the rest of the world, NASCAR, which has always moved fast, is moving even faster these days. Faster than ever, in fact.

In and around NASCAR, newness is everywhere you look. Newness is *anywhere* you look.

Look first at NASCAR headquarters in Daytona Beach, Florida. There's a new man in charge, in the town where going fast is a way of life. A new CEO/Chairman, actually. Brian France—grandson of NASCAR founder "Big Bill" France Sr., son of the man who turned a sport into an industry, Bill France—has jumped into the driver's seat of America's most popular form of motorsports.

Bill France, no longer at the wheel, rides shotgun still. Much like when his father handed over the reins thirty years ago then hung close, so too will *this* Bill France. He's down the hall, not out the door. The new boss was reminded of this up-front by the old boss in what amounted to NASCAR tough love.

Said Brian: "Bill told me that I'd have to produce, or else we'd have to make a change."

Brian France already has produced. NASCAR offices in New York City and Los Angeles reflect his influence and his *own* vision. Ditto for the epic television deal that began in 2001 and immediately took NASCAR to millions of new fans across the country.

He also was heavily involved in the 2003 negotiations to find a new entitlement sponsor of NASCAR's premier series. Early in 2003, R.J. Reynolds announced that it would end its groundbreaking sponsorship of the NASCAR Winston Cup Series after thirty-three years. By summertime, NASCAR had a new sponsor lined up, Nextel Communications.

The NASCAR Nextel Cup Series started this year. How's that for new? How's that for producing?

The concept of newness is spilling over into the business of schedule making. "Realignment 2004 and Beyond" is the label attached to the schedule changes, a plan outlined by Bill France at the start of 2003. The plan is based on the realities of an ever-expanding NASCAR fan base, no longer a primarily Southeastern situation.

Realignment is all about geographical balance, all about exposure. More places equal more fans—a simple equation for long-term success of America's most popular spectator sport.

Starting in 2005, California Speedway, Texas Motor Speedway, and Phoenix International Raceway *all* will have two NASCAR Nextel Cup races. Relatively new events in Chicago, Las Vegas, and Kansas City also exemplify NASCAR's expansion mode.

North Carolina Speedway no longer will be on the schedule. Also in 2005, Darlington (South Carolina) Raceway will have only one event.

As Bill France likes to say, "You can't stand still, or else you might get passed up."

Hard to imagine NASCAR being passed. Especially these days.

Newness is evident in the rulebook, newness aimed at improving the competition and safety on the race track, all with an eye toward cost-containment. The competition, after all, is the core product, the reason there are events worth realigning. Aerodynamics are constantly being addressed, as are tire compounds. These developments result, partly, from NASCAR listening to its drivers and fans, then looking in the mirror.

New, fresh faces are coming to NASCAR all the time, making even the one time "Wonder Boy," Jeff Gordon, seem like an elder statesman by comparison. Jimmie Johnson, Kurt Busch, Kevin Harvick, Ryan Newman, Kasey Kahne—they're the leaders of the cadre of "young guns" who are energizing the sport.

Dale Earnhardt Jr. is considered a "tweener" by some: too old to be grouped with the twenty-somethings, but by no means a true veteran. Still, he is universally recognized as the unofficial leader of the "new NASCAR" among the competitors, taking up where his late father left off.

Brian France—call him a young gun, too. He is, as CEOs go, having turned forty-two in August 2004. Call him, also, the standard-bearer of NASCAR newness. When all is said and done, years from now, he likely will be considered a pioneer of sorts, just like his grandfather and father.

"What people may notice that's different about me is that I like to get things done," Brian France said. "We're going to get things done. We're going to move fast."

For these times, it's an appropriate mantra.

ACKNOWLEDGEMENTS

The authors of this book would like to gratefully acknowledge the following people for helping to make this book possible: NASCAR chairman and CEO Brian France; NASCAR vice president Jim Hunter; the staff at Motorsports Images and Archives—Eddie Roche, Nancy Kendrick and Shanna Harbuck; Jon Schreiner—ISC Publications; Mike Skinner; Raymond Parks; Fred Lorenzen; Owen Kearns; Kerry Gilbert; Lee Packard; Dr. John Craft; Jim Hoersting; Cindie Reid; and Bob Bradley.

NOTES

Chapter 1

1. William Neely, *Daytona USA* (Tuscon: Aztec Corp, 1979), 45.

2. Bill Tuthill. 1973. Interview by Buz McKim.

3. Raymond Parks. April 2004. Interview by Buz McKim.

Chapter 2

4. Sylvia Wilkinson, *Dirt Tracks to Glory* (Chapel Hill: Algonquin Books, 1983), 27.

5. Dale Earnhardt. "GNI Interview: Dale Earnhardt" by Steve Waid. *Grand National Scene*, March 1983, 10.

6. Bill France Jr. February 2001. Interview by Bob Zeller.

Chapter 3

7. Fred Lorenzen. June 1993. Interview by Buz McKim.

8. David Pearson. 1980. Interview by Jim Hunter.

9. Bill France Sr. "The Boycott of Talladega" by Gene Granger. *American Racing Classics*, July 1993, 19.

Chapter 4

10. David Pearson. 1980. Interview by Jim Hunter.

11. Jade Gurss, *DW: A Lifetime Going Around in Circles* (New York: Penguin Group (USA) Inc., 2004), 160.

12. Cale Yarborough. *Grand National Scene*, "NMPA Taps Cale Yarborough as Driver of the Year," January 19, 1979.

Chapter 5

13. Darrell Waltrip. Column titled "Bob Myers" by Bob Myers. *Stock Car Racing Magazine*, March 1982, 20.

14. Bill Elliot, "The Weather's Hot and–Yep–So is Bill Elliott" by Steve Waid, *Grand National Scene*, May 7, 1987, 16.

15. Dale Earnhardt Jr. February 2004. From a press conference held in the Daytona International Speedway media center following the 2004 Daytona 500.

Chapter 6

16. Bill Elliot, *NASCAR Winston Cup Yearbook–1992* (Charlotte: UMI Publications, Inc., 1992), 208.

17. Jeff Gordon. August 1994. From a press conference following the 1994 Brickyard 400.

18. Dale Earnhardt, "Sweet Vindication" by Jeff Owens, *NASCAR Winston Cup Scene*, February 26, 1998, 58.

19. Bill France. "NASCAR Announces Race Planned for Japan" by John Griffin. *NASCAR News*, December 6, 1995, 1.

ABOUT THE AUTHORS

ABOUT THE ARCHIVES

H.A. (Herb) Branham comes by his love of auto racing naturally. He was born in Indianapolis, and lived only a mile away from the city's famed racetrack.

Prior to becoming a Communications Manager with the NASCAR NEXTEL Cup Series in 2001, Branham was assistant sports editor at the *Tampa (Florida) Tribune*, where he had previously covered auto racing for fifteen years. Branham won several writing awards while at the *Tribune*; in 1997, he was a finalist in the Associated Press Sports Editors (APSE) feature-writing category, with a story that was deemed one of the top ten in the nation that year. He is the author of the 1996 book *Sampras: A Legend in the Works*, which details the career of tennis great Pete Sampras. Branham lives in Ormond Beach, Florida, with his wife Catherine and their four children.

Buz McKim hails from Hackensack, New Jersey, and was virtually born into the sport of auto racing. His father owned cars that competed in NASCAR's Sportsman and Modified divisions on Northeastern racetracks in the early 1950s. McKim grew up around racing with his father changing roles from car owner to race announcer. Later, McKim attempted a driving career, but found it was more profitable to paint the numbers on the cars instead.

He pursued a career in commercial art, designing many paint schemes for cars in NASCAR's premier series during the 1970s, including the 1975 and 1976 Daytona 500-winning cars. McKim later developed a line of limited-edition racing prints dealing with historical NASCAR moments.

Always a historian, McKim became Director of Archives for International Speedway Corporation in January 1999. McKim accepted the position of Historic Database Coordinator with the NASCAR Public Relations Department in September 2003, where he still deals with the history of the sport he loves.

Motorsports Images and Archives is one of the world's premier repositories of racing-related film, video, and memorabilia. Located in Daytona Beach, Florida, the Archives represents more than one hundred years of racing history dating back to the first land-speed record time trials held on the hard-packed sands of Ormond Beach.

With the establishment of NASCAR in the late 1940s, to the building of Daytona International Speedway, the "World Center of Racing" in the late 1950s, the "Archives" expanded along with the monumental growth of American Motorsports. The collection continues to grow as a team of professional photographers representing MI&A travels to the premier race tracks around the country capturing the moments that captivate race fans the world over.